I Am
Potential

I Am Potential

Eight Lessons on Living, Loving, and Reaching Your Dreams

Patrick Henry Hughes

with Patrick John Hughes and Bryant Stamford

Da Capo
∞
LIFE
LONG

HAMPSTEAD PUBLIC LIBRARY
9 MARY E CLARK DRIVE
HAMPSTEAD, NH 03841

A Member of the Perseus Books Group

Copyright © 2008 by
Patrick Henry Hughes, Patrick John Hughes, and Bryant Stamford

Alternate editions for the visually impaired are available through Benetech at www.benetech.org.

DESIGN BY JANE RAESE
Set in 11-point Sabon

Cataloging-in-Publication Data for this book is available from the Library of Congress.

First Da Capo Press edition 2008
ISBN 978-0-7382-1298-2

Published by Da Capo Press
A Member of the Perseus Books Group
www.dacapopress.com

Da Capo Press books are available at special discounts for bulk purchases in the United States by corporations, institutions, and other organizations. For more information, please contact the Special Markets Department at the Perseus Books Group, 2300 Chestnut Street, Suite 200, Philadelphia, PA 19103, or call (800) 810-4145, ext. 5000, or e-mail special.markets@perseusbooks.com.

2 4 6 8 9 7 5 3 1

To Granddaddy—I miss you

Contents

Foreword

Blessed are the peacemakers,
for they will be called sons of God.
— MATTHEW 5:9

I have seen firsthand the power of Patrick Henry Hughes to transform tens of thousands in an instant. And the beauty of it is, all who were present, including Patrick Henry, were unaware of what was taking place.

I'm a big University of Louisville Cardinals fan, and I always attend the home football games. The first time I witnessed Patrick Henry "marching" with the Louisville band at halftime, I admit I choked up. There he was, sitting in his wheelchair and playing the trumpet while his father expertly guided him through the halftime marching routine, meshing perfectly with the other two-hundred-plus band members as they crisscrossed the field.

The transforming event took place in November 2006, during a football game between the University of Louisville and a major Big East conference rival. Sitting in the visitors' section across the aisle from me were five thousand rowdy fans, many of them wearing sweatshirts painted with nasty phrases about Louisville. They were throwing ice and debris into our section, not to mention the fighting words laced with obscene gestures coming our way.

During TV timeouts, their group booed whenever the announcer introduced individual Louisville student athletes who were being honored for academic achievement and professors and others cited for outstanding service. At halftime, when the marching band made its way onto the field, these fans booed even louder, drowning out their music.

Their fans seemed determined to push a confrontation. And many on the Louisville side were eager to accommodate them. As the halftime show was winding down, it was announced that Patrick Henry Hughes would perform. There was excitement, then grumbling among the Louisville faithful. The sentiment was strong that if those surly fans booed Patrick Henry and drowned out his performance, there would be war.

You could feel the tension build as we waited.

As Patrick Henry appeared on the giant TV screen in the end zone, the camera zoomed in for a close-up. He struggled briefly with his sunglasses, and I glanced over at the visitors section.

Their fans had no idea who Patrick Henry was or what to expect. All they could see was a young man in a band uniform seated at a keyboard: nothing terribly unusual about that. Yet, something must have told them this was a special moment. Suddenly, all was quiet as he leaned forward, ready to play.

There was a brief hesitation, and then Patrick Henry's fingers danced across the keyboard and launched into the Ray Charles hit "What'd I Say."

The moment he began, the entire place erupted. Everyone

was clapping and cheering wildly—and to my astonishment, the positive response from the rival fans matched the intensity of Louisville's. As Patrick Henry performed on the big screen, I watched in wonder as the aggressive, tough guys who were threatening us moments ago now smiled and gave the Louisville fans two thumbs up. Fans on both sides were actually exchanging high-fives across the aisle.

Impending war had morphed seamlessly into loving peace. We all were united, a massive family bonded briefly in our appreciation and respect for this extraordinary young man who had overcome so much. It was truly beyond comprehension to me, but as I would later learn, it was typical in the world of Patrick Henry Hughes.

Everyone in the stadium was touched that night, and for a fleeting moment, one holy instant, we communicated on a deeper level than what we rarely get to visit in our daily lives. Ever so slightly, and perhaps only quite briefly, we were changed.

My first meeting with Patrick Henry Hughes, face to face, was equally and inexplicably powerful. He and his dad, Patrick John Hughes, came to my home for a visit. I write a column for the *Louisville Courier-Journal* and had devoted my Thanksgiving Day column to that football game. Patrick John and I had been e-mailing back and forth ever since. Patrick Henry wanted to write a book, and we were meeting to discuss my helping him with the project. I had my doubts if I'd have time, mostly because my plate was overflowing with obligations that kept me running night and day.

Over the years, I have come to appreciate that sometimes the most incredible things happen when it appears nothing at all is going on. This was one of those occasions. Dad wheeled Patrick Henry onto my back porch. The young man greeted me, we shook hands, and for some reason, I held his hand longer than is customary. Yet he smiled at me and seemed perfectly comfortable that I was holding on. I know now that touch is so important to him as a primary source of information.

There are those among us who are able to touch us genuinely, to instantly disarm us, and in so doing allow communication soul to soul. Patrick Henry is one of these rare individuals. He is gifted in many ways, but he also possesses an innocence that, even from a distance, reaches out so unconditionally, you are moved to respond in kind. And somehow, this intimate contact with someone you've never met before seems like the most natural thing in the world.

When I met Patrick Henry that day, there was a profound sense of familiarity surrounding him. I felt as if I had known him all my life. When I held his hand and heard his voice, I knew something I hadn't a moment ago. I realized I would learn from him.

Patrick Henry Hughes is unique, and not just because he was born with a basketful of infinitely rare physical disabilities. On the contrary, he's unique because of his amazing attitude about it. He told me, "I'm blind and I live my life in a wheelchair, so some people might feel that, 'Gee, what a terrible thing to have to live like that.' But I don't see it that way. When I go to bed at night and count my blessings, I have a long list to get through." Ask him about his disabilities, and he'll be quick to tell you, "What disabilities? People who are disabled can't do things. I *can* do things—whatever I set my mind to. My mom and dad raised me that way." These are not just words put together in a sound bite to attract attention. They are Patrick Henry's credo, his philosophy of life.

This book is not only the story of Patrick Henry's life, but also a guide for those who seek to live their own life to the fullest each day. In getting to know Patrick Henry and the Hughes family, and watching their impact on others, several distinct, core elements emerged to help explain who he is and why he has been able to rise above profound adversity. These elements form the basis for the eight lessons on living with faith and without fear, loving unconditionally, and reaching your dreams—no matter how unattainable they may seem.

Patrick Henry Hughes is truly a blessing to our world and an example of the potential that lives within us all.

—*Bryant Stamford*

A Note from Patrick Henry

Before I get into my story, I need to tell you how it's organized so you won't get confused. I will be telling a lot of the story, but you also will be hearing from my dad, Patrick John Hughes. We let you know when the voices change with headings: *Patrick Henry* or *Dad*. We've used "Dad," rather than "Patrick John," because our names are so similar.

I Am
Potential

Chapter 1

When Life Gives You Lemons, Accept Them and Be Grateful

God, give us grace to accept with serenity
the things that cannot be changed,
Courage to change the things which should be changed,
And the Wisdom to distinguish the one from the other.
— REINHOLD NIEBUHR

My name is Patrick Henry Hughes, and I came into this world on March 10, 1988. My birthday should have been the best day ever for my mom and dad, but it turned out to be a pretty rough one. The day after my birthday was even worse.

Dad had gone home to shower and shave, then came back to the hospital and arrived at Mom's room just as the pediatrician walked in. Mom says the doctor seemed nervous and kept looking down at a chart he was holding tightly with both hands. Then he'd look at me curled up in her arms. When the doctor started talking, his voice broke and he had to stop and clear his throat.

I

There were problems. The medical team had learned some things about my health, but there was still a lot they didn't know and they'd need to do more tests.

After what seemed like forever, the doctor told them my condition looked as if it could be dwarfism. "X-rays suggest it might be short-limb dysplasia and a disproportionate truncated structure," he explained. Dad asked him to speak English.

"The arms and legs are shorter than you would expect by looking at the rest of his body. That's one problem . . ." He paused and checked his chart again. "And there's more." He waited for my parents to give him the go-ahead.

"I'm sorry to be the one to tell you. Your baby has inherited an extremely rare condition. He doesn't have eyes."

My mother had thought I was just taking my time before I opened my eyes. When Mom recalls that day, she says the doctor's words were like being socked in the stomach, because she lost her breath.

The doctor continued, "I regret to say there's still more you need to know . . . when you're ready." And then there was another seemingly interminable pause. When he continued, both Mom and Dad couldn't believe their ears.

Dad held my mom and me. "It's not fair!" Mom sobbed. "I did everything I could to make sure our baby would be healthy." Dad wondered, Why would God do this to us? Thankfully, God gave him the answer a few years later.

On the day I was born, you might say I arrived carrying a bag full of lemons, not the kind of thing my family had in mind. I think they would have preferred oranges; they're sweeter and have less bite. But life is what it is and you just have to keep going. You can't change lemons into oranges, no matter how hard you try. But just because you can't do that doesn't mean you give up. Mom and Dad taught me you have to hang in there and learn to deal with what happens to you. And once you do, you discover that lemons are pretty cool and you can make something better out of them, like lemon meringue pie. One of my favorites.

My parents were my earliest and best teachers. But before they could teach me about acceptance, they had to learn it themselves. It wasn't easy, and to hear them tell it, they had to go through a crash course that started with letting go of their hopes and dreams, and especially their dreams for me.

Pretty tough, but you can't move forward unless you're willing to accept where you are.

At the moment I was born, Dad didn't know what to expect. Maybe he didn't expect anything, because he was so caught up with the emotions. All he knows is the first words he heard were not the predictable, "Congratulations, you are the proud parents of a healthy baby boy!" Instead, at first, nobody said anything, and it got really quiet. Kind of strange, he thought. Then he heard something about "multiple anomalies." He always likes to joke, so he asked, "What the heck are those?" But at the time, he really didn't know.

He watched the doctor and nurses off to the side talking among themselves, but he didn't ask them what was going on, not wanting to appear ignorant or as if he were meddling in their business. After all, he'd seen fingers and toes and all the right stuff he could take in during the brief, hectic moment I came into the world. I was his first child, so he assumed the word "anomaly" must be some generic medical term that applied to newborns.

Dad watched while the nurse wiped me off, wrapped me up in blankets, and gave me to Mom. My eyelids were closed, and my mother thought I looked like all the other newborn babies she'd ever seen. She gets emotional when she talks about back then. "I just loved holding you and wanted to keep us right there, just like we were," she told me. But after only a minute, the staff told her they needed to get me to the nursery right away. She didn't like it one bit, but she assumed they knew best and held her tongue, which if you know my mom wasn't an easy thing for her. Especially when it came to me.

Meanwhile, Dad was more awake and alert, and the more he saw going on, the more he began to question whether the activity was routine. He was told to hurry to the nursery, but when he got there, they made him wait outside. As he waited, he became increasingly concerned about why they separated me from Mom so quickly. Shouldn't there be some sort of bonding process going on right after birth? And there was a flurry of doctors coming and going, rushing right past him as though he wasn't standing there. He tried to catch somebody's eye, hoping one of the staff would stop and tell him something, but they just kept going. With each passing minute, Dad's fear grew.

Back in the delivery room, Mom was tired. She felt horrible and wonderful at the same time, if that's possible. She always tells me she wanted a boy to be her first. I know my dad had big dreams about playing baseball with me—he's a fan of all sports, golf, basketball, and football, but loves baseball the most. My mother just lay there with her eyes closed, picturing us in the backyard: Dad going all out the way he always does, putting down bases to create the perfect field. I'd be catching the ball and tossing it back. I remember hearing about the movie *Field of Dreams* and thinking Dad was probably like the star, Kevin Costner. He'd build the field and they would come, his and Mom's first son, then their second and third. Mom shared that dream, too, with a tomboy daughter thrown into the mix somewhere.

Mammaw Betty (my grandma—Mom's mother) arrived to sit with Mom while Dad went with me. Dad liked to say Mom had a textbook pregnancy. But Mom remembers that day in the hospital when she felt what she calls her "mother's instincts"—something wasn't quite right, but she couldn't put her finger on it exactly.

After resting awhile, Mom called for the nurse, asking for me. When they finally brought me back to her and she held me, everything seemed normal again. She examined me: My eyes were still closed, which seemed natural enough for a baby just a few hours old. Dad returned, and they squeezed each of my fingers and toes. Everything checked out. She started to feel better, and she and Dad were able to have a "family moment." Later that evening, the nurse who came to take me back to the nursery told my parents they'd get a full report from the pediatrician the next day.

The next morning, the nurse had brought me back to Mom, who noticed that my eyes were still closed. That's when the doctor walked in to talk with my parents and told them I didn't have any eyes. And he explained the details about the rest of my problems.

"Your baby's legs are deformed, and though it's too early to tell, he may never be able to walk. And his arms . . . they're deformed, too, and he may not be able to use them the way other people do."

The doctor wasn't finished yet and was about to go on, but Mom held up her hand. She didn't care what the rest was—she needed time to digest what he had told her about my eyes. She stared at my face.

After a few moments, my parents decided they had to know everything, and it might as well be now. "Go ahead," my dad said quietly.

"The damage to your son could be more than physical, but we won't know for sure and to what extent for quite a while." That was too much for Mom. Although she was overwhelmed with all my physical problems, to add mental problems to the list was more than she could bear right then. Dad told the doctor they needed to be alone.

My parents would later learn that I didn't have mental disabilities, which was the good news. All the rest at the time seemed to be really terrible. Mom didn't want to blame the doctor, but she decided he didn't know what he was talking about when he said my problems were permanent. It couldn't be this bad. God wouldn't let this happen. Right then, Mom decided that if there was a way to fix my problems, she'd find it, no matter what.

When it was time for Mom to leave the hospital, she couldn't take me with her. On top of everything, I was jaundiced. The doctors told her jaundice is common in new babies and it probably wasn't that serious. But I had to be isolated from the other babies, because the doctors were unsure if it could be a sign of hepatitis. They also reported they'd have to call in a specialist to do more blood tests. Just one more thing to worry about.

My parents remember those first days as a slow-motion nightmare. Of course, they wanted information, and the more the better. Most of all, my mom wanted something positive to hold on to, but there was nothing yet. No eyes, arms and legs that didn't work right, jaundice, and possible mental disabilities. What other shoes were about to drop? Worse, Mom didn't know what was definite, because it was too early to confirm the diagnoses they'd made. The physicians spoke to her as if they were giving her facts, then they'd say, "Of course, this is all speculation until we run more tests."

Mom remembers thinking, if my baby has so many problems, will he be strong enough to make it? If not, is it best that a baby with so many problems is freed from suffering? She began wondering about the tests they had done months ago, the ultrasound, because it had given no hint of what I would bring with my birth. What if she and Dad had known about my condition in advance? They don't believe in abortion, but would they have done anything differently?

There's no way to answer such a question, but I've always known my parents loved me, no matter what. By not knowing what they would face, they had been delivered from making impossible choices. "It's another example," Mom said, "of how sometimes the best blessings can be right in front of you, but you don't see them, because you forget that God is always there, working things out behind the scenes."

When she was finally able to bring me home after the jaundice thing cleared up, Mom felt better, but she knew she faced a steep mountain ahead. Lots of folks came by to visit and see me, and one of Mom's friends who knew all about what was going on with me told her, "God never gives you more than you can handle. Trust that, and trust God." In her heart, Mom knew her friend was right. Another friend told my mother that she had to move on with her life, and to do that, she'd have to first accept what is. "You have to give up your expectations." Mom didn't like that one, but she knew it was right, too.

Dad was trying hard to stay strong about everything, but it wasn't really working. Those earliest days of my life were the hardest of Dad's. He's used to dealing with problems head-on and pushing until he solves them or makes them better. In this case, he could do nothing to change my disabilities, and he felt useless.

After nights of exhaustion from worrying about me, Mom suddenly felt at peace. This feeling seemed to come out of nowhere: She knew in her heart that for some reason, she was meant to have a baby like me, with challenges to overcome. We were meant to be a family. She was blessed with what Dad calls fierce determination and would dedicate herself completely to making sure I got everything I needed to not only survive, but also to live a good life, no matter what the odds. She didn't know how they'd do it yet. The only thing she knew for sure was that before she could move forward, she had to accept what God had given her and trust that someday she'd know why and be thankful for all of it.

DAD

I've been blessed more than anyone can imagine, and my son, Patrick Henry, is a big part of that. We have attracted a lot of attention lately and get thousands of e-mails. Many of them praise me, and I'm humbled at the thought, especially when I think about who I was before Patrick Henry was born. My wife, Patricia, bore the lion's share of the burden, dealing with all the obstacles surrounding Patrick Henry's early years. I feel the need to tell you this right up front, because I don't want you to think of me as Super Dad, someone who easily and naturally stepped into the role. Later, I'll give you more details about my transformation and how Patrick Henry teamed up with God to change me in ways I would have thought impossible. But then, that's the miracle of my son from the very beginning.

I hadn't really thought a lot about having kids. Until I met Patricia, my life was pretty much about me. Then I fell in love, which tends to expand one's horizons, and for me, this meant becoming a father. But we fathers, especially on the first go-round, don't necessarily have an accurate picture of what parenting is about. If I'm typical, we have a tendency to skip right over all the hard parts. My vision of having kids was a flock of sons who loved sports. Ignoring images of the diaper years, teething, potty training, chicken pox, and so forth was easy for me; they never entered my mind. It was as if our first son was just going to march right out and onto the ball field, and we'd live happily ever after. No wonder our wives sometimes get a little put out with us daydreaming dads.

Pregnancy, of course, occupies a family in just about every way you can imagine. At first, it's exciting, dreaming about your first child, and Patricia took her pregnancy in stride like the trouper she is. But after several months, I know she was getting a little tired of being pregnant—and exasperated with me. My participating in the Lamaze classes was a big deal to her. But it seemed that when we arrived at the class and got comfortable, I just couldn't stay awake. Try as I might to avoid it, I'd soon be sleeping like our newborn to come. I had an excuse: I was sleep-deprived. I worked late shifts, but to be honest, I was also out doing too much stuff, entertaining myself as much as possible. Patricia accepted the first part, but she didn't much like the second, and she sure didn't like my sleeping in class.

I was familiar with what the Lamaze classes were trying to do, yet I had trouble accepting that I always had to be there. A small piece of the class was directed toward me, the dad—information on how I could be encouraging and supportive during labor, as if I weren't going to do this automatically. The rest was important, too, I knew, but what did it have to do with me? One class had to do with complications that could arise during labor and birth, and the kinds of medical interventions that might be needed. It was stuff I didn't want to hear and didn't see as relevant. Everything would be fine. It always was.

Finally, the time was near, and we started for the hospital. I wasn't like those husbands who panic and run out the front door with a suitcase, driving off and forgetting their wives. I was calm, if not a little distracted. Patricia likes to remind me of a little scene that points out pretty accurately how self-absorbed I was. And she's right. There we were, about to have a baby, but what was foremost on my mind? Sports. I like listening to sports talk radio, and since it was March, I was tuned in to anything that had to do with the NCAA basketball tournament. So, I kept my ear on the radio, even as I drove my laboring wife to the hospital.

I was lost in my own thoughts until we rounded the bend and came face-to-face with the hospital. I think that's the first time it hit me. I was going to be a dad! I was excited, though I tried not to show it. *Be cool* was my motto.

On the way into the hospital, I was supremely confident of the outcome; there was no reason to think otherwise. Patricia had done everything right. No smoking, no drinking. She ate the right foods and gained just the right amount of weight. Excellent prenatal care. And we had evidence. The midterm ultrasound showed nothing unusual. Now, in the hospital, they examined Patricia and decided this was the real thing. Our son was on his way!

I was determined to be the pillar of support for my wife. I studied everything in the labor room, all the gadgets she was hooked up to. The one that caught my eye was a machine that measures the frequency and intensity of contractions— not only predicting that a contraction is coming, but also measuring its strength. Sort of like a seismograph, which measures earthquake activity and converts it to conform to the Richter scale. I figured this would be helpful for me to tell her, but I quickly stopped these pronouncements when she made it clear that if I told her another *big* contraction was coming, she'd get out of bed and strangle me. It wasn't time for my cheerleading yet.

Patricia had wanted to have natural childbirth. As the birthing process continued, I think we both underestimated the amount of pain involved. I, of course, still have no idea, but judging from Patricia's face back then, I knew the pain was pretty steep. The doctor gave her an epidural, which gave her little relief. Now it was too late for any other interventions, and we headed for the delivery room.

It all happened so fast. Patricia started pushing, and before we knew it, Patrick Henry was born. Wow! It was a miraculous experience; the emotions surrounding the birth of your child, especially the first one, are overwhelming. Something deep inside is stirred, triggering emotions you never knew you had. My head was spinning.

At such moments, everything is intensified: Every view, every word, is vivid and sears its way into your memory. My senses told me everything was fine. I saw a baby who looked normal, heard a cry that sounded normal. But an odd feeling came over me, some weird combination of extreme joy and dread, as if I had the winning lottery numbers but realized I'd lost the ticket.

I took my wife's hand, congratulated her, and told her how proud of her I was. When I started to head toward the waiting room, knowing our families would want the news, I was told to go straight to the nursery. I was in a daze and simply followed where the staff pointed. As I left the room, I bumped into one of the doctors, who asked me if I wanted to pray with him. Having been raised a Catholic, I felt obliged to participate in prayer when it was offered. But I wasn't sure what we were praying about, other than to be thankful for the birth of my son. "Sure," I said, "I'd be glad to." We bowed our heads and prayed the Our Father. The doctor then patted me on the shoulder and reassured me all would be well. I thanked him.

I went to the nursery as instructed and kept my ears open for information. At this point, I still wasn't aware of what all the commotion was about—or even that there was anything seriously wrong with my son. Since I had no reference point for what was normal and how many doctors are consulted to look at a newborn, I took it that things were okay. I didn't want to jump to conclusions, and I wasn't about to burden Patricia unnecessarily, especially in her depleted state. Surely everything would turn out fine.

As time went on, it was harder and harder to assume all was well. What kind of expertise was required to look at a baby and decide whether he's whole or not? I walked back to my wife's room to await further word from the staff. With each passing minute, my optimism dropped, but I tried to still be upbeat with Patricia.

Gradually, piecing things together, it became clear my son had problems that were not typical. When I finally returned to the waiting room, family and friends were milling around, anxiously awaiting word. I had some news, but no details. I'd learned there were problems with my son's limbs and eyes, but I didn't know the severity or the prognosis. I was holding up pretty well at this point, trying to do my best John Wayne impersonation, and I assured everyone Patrick Henry would be fine. Then I saw my mother. I walked over to her and pulled her aside. Instantly, tears welled in my eyes, and I lowered my head to her shoulder and sobbed. I had a profound feeling of helplessness I had never before experienced. At some deep level, I think I knew things were far worse than I wanted to believe.

The next day, the doctors finally opened up and told us what they knew. Young Patrick Henry had an extremely rare combination of birth defects. The extent of all the defects wouldn't be clearly known for some time, and this was true even for the condition of his eyes.

Later on, I learned some things that helped put this time into perspective. We were being kept in the dark because the medical team was in the dark as well. I learned that doctors, strange as it may seem, may not recognize immediately that a baby is born without eyes. With every newborn, drops are applied to the eyes to prevent infection. The first hint of a problem may be that the drops do not sink in the way they're supposed to. The medical term for the condition is *anophthalmia,* which means the absence of the globe and ocular tissue—the eye. There is nothing in the orbit, because the eyes did not develop early in the pregnancy, perhaps as early as the first twenty-eight days. When both eyes are missing, it is called *bilateral anophthalmia,* an extremely unusual occurrence. Congenital anophthalmia can occur alone, or in combination with other birth defects. Patrick Henry had inherited a combination that was extraordinarily rare. Why us, Lord?

Those first several days were the hardest, hearing my wife cry herself to sleep. She'd lie there and I could hear her whimper, "It's not fair. It's so unfair." I tried my best to comfort her, feeling useless. It was the worst experience of my life, but I hid my grief from those around me, trying to appear strong.

One of the hardest things was having to let go of my dream that my son and I would someday play baseball in the backyard. My plans to set up a baseball diamond, complete with the backstop I intended to construct from two-by-fours and chicken wire, were not to be realized—at least for now. There would be other babies, wouldn't there? Other sons to catch my throws? Or, would any other children be similarly afflicted? We had lots of questions, but no answers.

Through it all and in the darkest hours, I still never gave up the hope that everything would be all right. Maybe it was my extreme naïveté. Sort of like denying you are having a heart attack—all this pain in my chest must be something else, just indigestion. That may have been part of it, but I think there was something larger going on.

As I said, although I was raised a Catholic, I was never overly religious, and I can't say that faith had occupied an important part of my daily life. My relationship with God was more or less one of convenience. "Lord, I really screwed up here, and I'd appreciate your bailing me out again." Now, looking back, the hand of God was in this big time, and in those moments, He was comforting me and reassuring me. Maybe it was because for once my prayers weren't about me.

Above all, it soon occurred to me that nothing would be served by fighting against our fate. If this was it, so be it. *We'll survive.* No, we'll do more than that. *We'll do all we can to make the situation better.* I felt this in my heart, but I truly had no idea of the magnitude of the challenges we faced.

Patricia knew immediately, and went on to carry the ball, doing all she could for our son while tolerating my hanging around in the background. She was gentle with me, never complaining that I was less than I could and should be. It was like she knew I needed time to someday grow up and come through.

Despite my lack of maturity, and because of Patricia's strength and selfless dedication, we moved forward through those first difficult days together: the Hughes family with our beloved newborn son, Patrick Henry.

When Life Gives You Lemons, Accept Them and Be Grateful

PATRICK HENRY

I've known from an early age that I was dealt a hand in life different from the cards others got. That's okay, because I also learned God would help me play that hand if I was willing to accept what I was missing and be thankful for what I *can* do. Mom and Dad saw to that.

When I meet folks, they often ask me if I had trouble accepting my disabilities. I'm not sure they believe me when I say no, because they tell me they would be really angry, or sad, or bitter if they couldn't walk or if they lost their sight. Maybe so, but these days, I can't even imagine feeling that way.

At first, it's natural to wish we could change the past. "How wonderful life would be," we tell ourselves, "if only this or that had happened instead." But where does that kind of thinking get you? Nowhere, and worse, it keeps you stuck there. I can honestly say I've learned that lesson and I do accept my life as it is.

When I think about all I've been through, I'm pretty amazed at how well things have gone. Twenty years after the fateful day that I was born, I'm attending college, majoring in Spanish. I sing, play the piano and trumpet, and am a member of my university's marching band. I've been able to travel the world and meet thousands of people doing what I love most—performing music.

I have so much to be thankful for, but it sure wouldn't have been as great if it weren't for my family and all the friends I've made over the years. And especially my parents, who have loved me and supported me at every turn. Maybe if someone else were my mom and dad and they rejected me or felt sorry for me or for themselves, my life might have turned out differently. But I guess you could say I was blessed with exactly the right ones.

Chapter 2

Do All You Can
to Change What You Can

God helps those who help themselves.
—BENJAMIN FRANKLIN, *Poor Richard's Almanac*

PATRICK HENRY

Once my parents began to settle into their new life with me, they realized they needed a plan. But how do you know where to begin? They had so many questions that it would have been overwhelming if they didn't take it one day at a time. That's probably the best advice they received from anyone, and sometimes, it seemed they were living breath to breath—up one moment, down the next. Along the way, they also were trying to follow a piece of advice that came at them, again and again, from all sides—"let go completely and begin fresh." They knew this, and they both were trying, but when you've held a dream so close to your heart for so long, it's tough letting it go.

DAD

Even when Patrick Henry was still a very young baby, Patricia never wanted him to hear her cry. She didn't want him to know he was different from other children. Nor did she want him to think we cared about that. We had to put up a tough exterior, no matter what was going on inside. We felt if everyone treated Patrick Henry as this pitiful, blind cripple, then he would pity himself. There's no room for that. You only become more dependent and needy if you allow yourself to go in that direction. Not on our watch! Patrick Henry had to be strong, unafraid to make it in the world.

PATRICK HENRY

I had six major surgeries early in life. Throughout my childhood, it seemed we were at the pediatrician's office or the ophthalmologist's every week. Because I was born without eyeballs in my sockets, the bone structure didn't form the way it's supposed to. That meant if I was going to have prosthetic eyes put in, they had to first reshape the sockets, expanding them gradually, step by step. Then after that, I'd have to undergo a series of surgeries.

From the beginning, my parents had to learn how to research the answers to many questions. When you have a child with disabilities, everything, no matter how elementary it might seem, has a learning curve. Choices that might appear obvious, like prosthetic eyes, were not so clear back then. Even once they learned my options, Mom and Dad had no idea if it was best to go a particular route. Was it worth putting me through surgeries, and what would be the advantages? There was no Internet back then and no easy way to find information, so a lot of what happened depended on who you talked to and if you were lucky enough to locate the right expert.

Since bilateral anophthalmia is so rare, even my doctors seemed not to know quite where to start. We were referred to the Kentucky Eye Institute in Louisville, where we went regularly for examinations—but the visits seemed limited to just that, examination. Maybe it's because Mom and Dad didn't know the right questions to ask. Or, maybe the doctors were waiting for a change to happen, some sign to guide them to the next step. Either way, months went by with no progress.

At our last visit, when I was a little more than a year old, the institute referred us to a dentist. It didn't seem to make sense. A dentist?

It turned out that this dentist specialized in facial reconstruction of people who had been in accidents. Although his forte was the mouth area, the doctors who sent us thought maybe he could do something for my eyes. When we understood this, my parents held out hope that some progress could be made.

After the dentist made a mold of my face, he decided he didn't have the expertise to follow through with the reconstruction work on my eyes—a step that would prepare them for the prostheses. This failure made my parents more anxious than ever about what the so-called experts really knew about my condition and what they could do for me. Mom and Dad had allowed themselves to become cautiously optimistic, but now it seemed we had encountered another dead end. But as always, when things are bleakest, a helping hand reaches down from above precisely when you need it.

When I was fifteen months old, Dad and I appeared on the local annual Crusade for Children TV fund-raising special. Firefighters in greater Louisville always lead the way in collecting funds for the crusade, and Dad was a volunteer fireman. He held me in his arms and talked about all the good things the crusade does for schools, agencies, and hospitals, and how the money was used to benefit kids like me.

A nice lady from across the river in southern Indiana saw the broadcast and contacted my parents to tell them about an ocularist who specialized in making and fitting artificial eyes. This woman also had a child with anophthalmia and had been down the same road we were heading. Knowing how hard it was to get reliable information, she gave us a name and office location in Indianapolis. Mom and Dad now had something new to explore. Thank you, God!

This time, on our first visit, I was fitted with my first set of conformers. These are acrylic disks, like a small, hollow marble cut in half and attached to a stem for ease of removal from the eye. These conformers are gradually increased in size, which in turn increases the size of the orbit—the hollow space where the eye normally fits. As the size of the orbit increases, it allows for a sphere to be surgically implanted. The doctor explained that the polyethylene sphere, like the wooden arch supports in a coal mine, keeps the orbit from collapsing.

Because I was just a little baby, I don't remember any of this, but Dad says I cried the first time I had to be fitted. My mom cried, too, praying this was really the right thing to do. This process took roughly a year before I could undergo surgery for my first set of eyes.

The condition of my eye sockets, of course, was only one of the challenges. My parents also sought out orthopedic surgeons to see what could be done, if anything, to correct my arms, legs, and hips.

As with my eyes, it was obvious I had trouble with my arms and legs, but the exact problem wasn't clear. In my legs, the femurs (thighbones) are much shorter than they should be, which is why the physicians initially thought my condition might be dwarfism. But they soon discovered it was more complicated—my thighbones didn't fit into the ball-and-socket joints of my hips. My femurs were instead being held in place by the tissues surrounding them, rather than by their joints, which explains why my legs aren't stable and don't move well. The doctors figured there might be similar problems with my arm joints, too, preventing me from being able to fully extend my arms. "Never lift him by his arms," the doctors warned my parents. This could dislocate my shoulders.

When I was two months old, I was fitted with braces to help me straighten my arms. Dad says I looked so tiny and helpless in my braces, which looked like some sort of medieval torture device. I was supposed to wear them as much as possible, but my parents didn't want to restrict me too much, since I could hardly move in them. So, I'd wear the braces at night, and off and on during the day. When they were off, I could explore my surroundings a little more like a normal baby.

I had leg braces, too, but we didn't use them as often as the arm braces. Not only were they hard to put on and uncomfortable, but they didn't seem to be accomplishing much. I had to live this way in braces until the doctors decided I was ready for my first surgery.

Finally, when I was six months old, I went into the hospital to have surgery to improve the function in my legs. The doctors thought the surgery would require relocating my hip joints. My parents were told the two bones (the heads of the femurs and the sockets of the hips) simply would need to be brought together and fixed in place. It was major surgery, but the doctors were optimistic.

Mom and Dad had high hopes as they paced, fretted, and then paced some more around the hospital halls. I was in the operating room for hours, and they grew more fearful of the outcome with each passing minute. What was taking so long? Finally, after I had been in surgery for more than four hours, the surgeon came out and told them that I could not be operated on as planned.

"There are too many problems, too many anomalies to correct," he explained. "I'm very sorry." Dad hated that word—"anomalies."

The surgeons had discovered a bunch of problems they

hadn't anticipated. The femoral heads of my thighbones had not developed, which meant there was no ball for the ball-and-socket joint of the hip. But even if there were heads, it turned out the sockets were deformed, too, so it didn't matter. The only thing the doctors could do was place a metal pin in my hip to monitor bone growth. Although they knew the doctors were just doing their best, my parents were still frustrated that it took more than four hours of surgery to figure that out.

DAD

The results of the hip surgery were very disappointing, but once we got out of the hospital and returned home, we realized that good things were happening, too. Despite the obstacles, the challenges, Patrick Henry began to grow in his own unique ways. He loved nursery rhymes and delighted in our singing children's songs, and he particularly enjoyed humming the tunes. We had tapes that sang the alphabet, numbers, and phonics, which he listened to constantly. It also seemed that his speech was coming along pretty well. At six months, his grandfather informed us Patrick Henry spoke his first word, and the word was "granddaddy." I was skeptical. But then one day soon after Patricia picked him up from day care after work, he spoke: "Ran da-da." Maybe my dad really did hear him say his first word. Thankfully, our fears that he might have mental problems began to fade.

Our son was beginning to blossom. His personality was

quickly developing a strength that surprised us. When we put his braces on, they were restrictive and uncomfortable, but like a little soldier, he rarely cried or complained. When we told him he couldn't do something, like pick at his surgical stitches, he understood it immediately. He was like a tiny adult, and we didn't have to worry that every time we turned our backs, he'd be doing something he wasn't supposed to.

Patrick Henry was a happy baby who loved to laugh. Ever curious, he always wanted to reach out and learn more. And when he learned a new skill, like his initial triumphs on the piano, it was obvious he had a bit of the ham in him, loving the attention it brought. He was a fast learner whose mind soaked up everything that crossed his path. It was glorious to behold, and admittedly, we loved showing him off.

We had started going to a parents support group provided by Visually Impaired Preschool Services to help us cope and learn from other parents. There we met parents who faced problems that, to me, seemed much more severe than our own problems. I'm not sure why, because Patrick Henry had a more challenging combination of physical afflictions to cope with. At first, Patricia and I would share freely the wonderful things that were going on with our son, and each week, it seemed we had something new and exciting to share with the group. Yet after awhile, I began to feel like one of those obnoxious parents who goes on and on about his perfect child. Although a little bragging seemed justified, given all we had been through, we decided it was time to stop going and keep our joyful moments to ourselves.

PATRICK HENRY

After the failed surgery on my hips and legs came my first eye surgery. I was a little over two years old, and my parents were really optimistic about this one. I would have eyes! Maybe I couldn't see with them, but at least my face would appear normal to other people. As with all surgeries, there were risks. Yet, there also was the chance that without the prosthetic eyes, my face might change shape to compensate and might develop a sunken appearance. They sure didn't want that to happen.

The first eye surgery was successful. The doctors implanted a porous polyethylene sphere in each of my eye sockets, to stretch and shape the orbit and to stimulate bone growth. The seventeen-millimeter sphere was just the "training" sphere, because it wasn't actually big enough. In the future, I'd have a second operation to increase the size of the sphere. Eventually, when my sockets were ready, I'd have two hand-painted prostheses inserted that could be easily removed for cleaning and put back in.

After the operation, I had many stitches holding the spheres in place. On top of that, my eyelids had to be stitched shut to protect the spheres. Apparently, my face was just awful to look at. There was severe swelling, and my face was a rainbow of black and blue and yellow. For the first few days, the appearance of my face kept getting worse. But Mom and Dad weren't allowed to do anything for my face— no icing it or even cleaning off the layers of encrusted blood.

Dad told me I looked worse than any prize fighter he'd ever seen, much worse than Muhammad Ali's battered face after his second fight with Joe Frazier. As bad as I looked, I must have been uncomfortable, because Dad said I'd squint and grimace. My parents had to tell me I couldn't touch my eyes. Even if the stitches itched, I couldn't scratch them, because it might ruin the effects of the operation. So, for weeks after the surgery, I never touched them. Dad says that was amazing for a two-year-old. Somehow, I just did what I was supposed to do.

When I was almost four years old, I was ready for my second eye operation. But this time, things couldn't have been more different, and they didn't go well. The size of the sphere was increased from seventeen to twenty-one millimeters, but the sphere was too big and wouldn't stay in place. My parents were told that normally, portions of real eye tissue from a cadaver would be inserted to help hold the sphere, but because of the AIDS scare at the time, the surgeons decided to use synthetic material instead. It didn't hold, and then the surrounding area got infected. As if that weren't enough, I had a reaction to the anesthetic.

After the surgery, I was lethargic and not my typical self. I just sat there and wasn't interested in anything, not my musical tapes or my noisy toys. Our house was quiet, which was really unusual with me around. The first day after surgery, my parents figured I'd come out of it the next day; it was just an anesthesia hangover. But by the second day, I was still in a daze, as if the drug still hadn't worn off. In fact, I seemed to be getting worse. They were worried.

After two full days, my parents feared I was becoming dehydrated, because I didn't want to drink, and if they tried to make me, I'd throw up anything they put in my mouth, even water. All I wanted to do was sleep. They tried once more to get me to sip something, but no luck. By then, it was late in the day. Since they couldn't get hold of any of the doctors in Indianapolis, where the surgery was performed, we took off for a nearby hospital emergency room.

Because I wasn't bleeding or obviously violently ill, the intake nurse didn't see my condition as critical and they made us wait. Four hours later, a doctor came by the examination room. Dad told him I had just undergone surgery and, since then, hadn't had anything to eat or drink for two days. Worse, I was vomiting and, by now, had the dry heaves. Yet the doctor took a quick examination of me and said I'd be okay. With that, he walked out of the room.

Dad was furious. Just as he was just starting to leave the room to go after anyone he could find and complain, I took a sip of water. That stopped him, and he and Mom watched to see if I would hold it down. When I did, and drank some more, they were relieved, and we left to go home. But the relief was short-lived. Although I was drinking fluids and had stopped throwing up, two days later I was still in a stupor.

DAD

Back then, we three used to go out to dinner regularly with my parents. In the days after that ER visit, Patricia and I didn't want to go out to eat, but my parents insisted we all try. It would do us good to get out of the house, they said.

But they were wrong. It was dreadful. The five of us sat at one of our favorite restaurants—fried chicken and down-home cooking—our plates untouched. My mother and father were worried sick, especially my dad, and we could hardly speak. Patrick Henry was slumped in his high chair, his head lowered to one side, not talking or laughing like his usual self, not asking questions, not reaching out for his granddaddy. We all just sat there looking at our little boy, each person wrapped in his or her own private thoughts. My own were, *Will he ever be like he was before the operation? Was his brain damaged from the operation or the anesthesia? Please Lord, help him.* Four days can be a long time when you're going through something like this. I tried to appear like my typical optimistic self. "Just give it time," I said, but inside I was dying.

Before this point, there seemed to be a growing sense of balance in our world. My son had multiple "anomalies," and we had accepted that. It wasn't easy, but we could cope with the problems presented by his blindness and lack of mobility, because we were blessed in so many other ways. His attitude, his upbeat personality, his ability to learn, and, of course, his blossoming musical talent provided plenty of opportunities for gratitude. Sitting there now, observing my son, I thought about those folks we met in the support group at Visually Impaired Preschool Services. Were their children more this way, quiet and unresponsive, and if so, was this why they didn't have the kinds of things to share that we did? Had we been too proud of Patrick Henry's progress?

I tried to eat and set an upbeat example, but mostly I just picked at my food. Was it possible all the good things we had experienced with our son were now going to be taken away from us? Just like that, with the snap of a finger? I knew that in the grand scheme of things, we're never promised life is going to be fair, but this was going too far. At that moment, the comparison of what life had been like with Patrick Henry to what it might be was devastating.

Patricia and I tried not to look at each other as the collective sadness around the table threatened to overwhelm us. I could handle this on my own, but I knew if I looked in her eyes and saw her pain, I'd lose it. I think she felt the same way. We've had many dark hours, but this ranked right up there among the worst.

What a stupid idea, going out to eat, I thought. This was agony, being in public and trying to pretend everything was fine. I remember sitting there looking at my son, and how, in the next moment, everything then seemed to get eerily quiet. Strange, for a crowded restaurant.

I looked around and was about to say something about it when suddenly, it was as if God had thrown a switch. Patrick Henry raised his head and smiled.

Everyone gasped.

From that moment on, he was his old self again. Patrick Henry loves all kinds of vegetables, and at this restaurant, they serve the food country style, in big bowls. We scooped huge portions on my son's plate, and he ate every bit and wanted more. It was as if he'd been lost in the desert—he couldn't get enough of anything. The rest of us immediately got our appetites back, too, and we joined Patrick Henry in what turned out to be one of the greatest meals we've ever had.

It was a valuable lesson and reinforced how abundantly we had been blessed, having Patrick Henry in our lives. Maybe we were guilty of taking the good things he brought with him too much for granted, I thought. If so, you'd better believe we'd never do that again. He had become the center of our universe, and when that was taken away, a black hole had opened up. Now the sunshine was back, and we thanked God for everything associated with our son—every doctor's visit, every brace, every physical-therapy session, every surgery.

PATRICK HENRY

When we left the restaurant, my belly was full and I was my old self again. Later that year, since my second eye operation had failed and the twenty-one-millimeter sphere didn't hold, I required a third eye operation for a nineteen-millimeter sphere. I also had to undergo surgery to correct an undescended testicle. After what we had just experienced, these last two operations scared my family. The doctors assured us that the anesthesia reaction was unusual and wasn't at all likely to occur again. So we went into the operations with hope and confidence that all would be well, and they were indeed successful. But that's not the end of the story.

The doctors felt they ultimately would need to increase the size of the sphere from nineteen to twenty-two millimeters, which would require a fourth operation when I was older. Mom and Dad had to give that a lot of thought. Should they put me through another eye operation, knowing the kinds of things that could go wrong? They always wanted to do everything they could to make my life better, but in this case, was it really necessary? They prayed hard about it and decided that putting me through another eye surgery just to get a better cosmetic appearance wasn't the right thing to do.

Now that my eye situation was settled and I seemed to be improving, my parents revisited any possibility that something could be done for my arms, hips, and legs. Every year, there are new medical breakthroughs that previously seemed impossible. What if just such a thing had happened in the years since my first operation, when I was six months old? Maybe there were new hip sockets that could be implanted to accept new heads that doctors would attach to my thighbones. My parents knew that this idea was reaching pretty far, but they always dreamed of a chance.

After much searching, they found no promising developments. What's more, my doctors didn't want to give them false hope.

So, it was time to accept that I'd probably never walk or stand on my own. I think I already knew this, and I hoped my acknowledging it would make it easier on my parents.

They tried to make out like my condition was no big deal, but I could tell that below the surface, they were sad to admit that nothing else could be done.

Nor did we ever hold out much hope for changing my arms in any meaningful way. But that's okay, because I can use them just fine to play my instruments and to feed myself, which are the things that are most important to me.

When we go back in time and talk about those days, I can hear the pain in Dad's voice. But then he quickly shifts gears and says if I were able to walk, I wouldn't be in a wheelchair, and he'd never have had the pleasure of pushing me around a football field at halftime, which ultimately benefited our family in so many ways. No matter how you look at it, it's all good.

DAD

When Patrick Henry was still very young, Patricia and I were concerned about having more children. Just how big were the risks? We decided to consult a geneticist to see if we could determine what the future might bring if we conceived again.

We learned that the exact incidence of anophthalmia is unknown, although some data indicate the prevalence of microphthalmia (small eyes) to be one in ten thousand. Bilateral anophthalmia (both eyes missing) is rarer still. It can be present at birth or acquired later in life as a degenerative condition. It can occur alone or, more rarely, in conjunction with other birth defects. Researchers currently are working hard trying to locate the gene or genes involved with the developing eye.

After a few visits, it was determined that both Patricia and I carry the same rare recessive gene, and it was a fluke that both hit at the same time. The geneticist did some analyses surrounding Patrick Henry's conditions and published a scientific report that the combination of his anomalies was so unique and extremely rare that other cases were unknown. The good news—and it seemed good to us, because we wanted to have more children—was that the odds that what happened to Patrick Henry would happen again were tiny at best.

Three years after Patrick Henry's birth, our second son, Jesse, was born. And four years after that, our third son, Cameron, came along. All three are as different as they can be, each wonderful in his own way.

Thankfully, finally, we thought we were out of the woods with Patrick Henry. Five surgeries in just his first few years on this earth were more than enough to last a lifetime. We had run the gauntlet and survived, and we were feeling pretty good about ourselves and Patrick Henry's situation. Then we found out he had to have another surgery.

PATRICK HENRY

My last surgery, at age ten, was on my back, because of scoliosis. When viewed from the back, the vertebrae in your spinal column should form a perfectly straight line from top to bottom. In my case, my spinal column snakes from left to right in an S shape. I had problems because I sat all the time, and since I don't have hip joints, I'm basically sitting on my spine. The scoliosis caused some pain, but not the worst I'd experienced. So I thought I could handle it indefinitely. But the doctor said the condition was getting worse and if I didn't have surgery, it could get so bad it would affect my lungs and I might not be able to breathe. Obviously, that's pretty serious, but when Dad told me it might get to where I couldn't sit up to play the piano, I really wanted to get the operation done.

I was also excited about another benefit of the surgery—being taller. The doctor said that after the operation, when my back was straighter, I would gain four inches in height. That would take me to exactly four feet tall. Why was that such a big deal to me at the time? I love to go to amusement parks and ride the rides; it's a blast. But a lot of rides wouldn't let me on, because I wasn't tall enough. You have to be a minimum of forty-eight inches tall to go on the roller coasters at Six Flags Kentucky Kingdom or Kings Island. That extra four inches meant the world to me, and I couldn't wait.

This might surprise some folks that I'm a bit of a dare-devil, or that the park would let me go on rides at all. There has never been a problem getting on the less scary rides, because there's no height requirement. All they require is that I'm able to get into the seat and strap on my seat belt. Dad does this all the time for me, no problem. As for the big roller coasters, I'd always wanted to feel the acceleration of racing downhill and experience going head over heels in the loop-de-loop, especially from the front seat. I had never thought it would be possible, because I was too short, but fixing my spine would finally remove that hurdle.

Mom and Dad drove me to the hospital on a cold and snowy day in January. We got there early, and the worst part for me was knowing I couldn't eat for a long time before the surgery because of the anesthetic. I think I love to eat more than just about anything, besides playing music, of course, and my parents know that. (Dad says I've never met a food I didn't like. That's not true. I don't like corn nuts, eggnog, Cream of Wheat, or sardines. But other than that, bring it on.) I love everything Mom cooks; she's fantastic. My favorite is chicken club rings. Dad calls these an instant heart attack, but they are delicious. They are a combination of mayonnaise, mustard, parsley, and onion, mixed with chicken, bacon, and cheese on crescent dough. Mom bakes them, then adds more cheese on top. And I don't have a sweet tooth—I have sweet *teeth*. Give me anything that's a dessert, and I'm happy.

When we arrived at the hospital, Mom checked the time and figured if we hurried, I could eat something and everything would still be okay. So she ran out and got Chinese food, one of my favorites. I tried not to eat too much, but it was hard resisting. I was nervous about the surgery, but this made everything better; it was as if we were having a picnic right there in the hospital.

The next morning, they put a mask over my face, and

when I breathed in, it smelled like fruit. I was looking forward to the dreams I'd have. Shortly after they told me to take some breaths and count backward, I was out like a light. When I woke up, I didn't remember a thing. All I knew was I felt as if I were wrapped in cement and couldn't move. Plus, I was thirsty. But the nurses said they couldn't give me anything to drink, so they let me suck on a little piece of ice.

The doctors had put two steel rods in my back to straighten it—that's major surgery. I was in the hospital ten days after the operation and pretty much just lay there in bed the first few days and listened to music. It was also the first and only time I can ever remember losing my appetite. Three bites of anything, like soup or broth, was enough. (Dad says I learned a brand new sentence: "I am full.") It was pretty tough, but I kept thinking that when I recovered, I'd get my first roller coaster ride, and that made it all worthwhile.

The nurse gave me a button to push for painkillers. It was attached to a thin IV hose that went from a plastic bag and into my arm. Mom said to use it when I needed to, but if I could help it, I shouldn't use it too much, so I tried not to press it. But moving at all was pretty awful, and I had to be turned over every hour so that I would heal properly, so I'd push the button a few times. Then the nurse told me I must have a high pain tolerance, because when other folks have this kind of back operation, they sometimes push that button a hundred times or more.

On the third day, the staff got me up for the first time and put me in a wheelchair, where I had to sit for five minutes.

This started my rehab process, and sitting up was the first task I had to tackle. It doesn't seem like a lot, I know, but it was an ordeal. Being moved was bad, but sitting was worse. The pain shot through my back and all the way down my legs, like a shock wave. The next day, I pretended I had to go to the bathroom right away, before my five minutes was up, so that I could get back into bed. When the nurse took the empty bedpan away, Mom made it clear she knew what I was up to and that my game wasn't going to work the next time.

Through it all, my parents made sure I was never alone, rotating shifts with my grandparents at all times. Once, Mom apologized that she had to leave for a little while. She told me she had to go home so that my brothers, Jesse and Cameron, would still be able to recognize her!

Finally, after the longest ten days of my life, it was my last day and I could go home. But first, I had to go to X-ray. It seemed like a long trip in the wheelchair, way more than the five minutes I was used to. We didn't take the IV with me, because we were leaving as soon as we finished the X-rays. I was already uncomfortable when we got there, and then I had to sit on a stool while they took the X-rays. The stool had no back or anything else for me to lean on. I've had pain of one sort or another all my life, but this was the worst I've ever felt. It was like daggers being jagged into my spine from top to bottom. I definitely wished I now had that button to push. The worst part was Mom's knowing I was in pain. When she met me after I was wheeled out of the X-ray room, she was crying so hard it broke my heart.

Once back home, I finally got my old wheelchair back, which was a big improvement. The one in the hospital had a giant seat, which propped up my legs so that they sort of stuck straight out, and that hurt. At home, my legs could dangle, which eased the pain a lot. I was supposed to be sitting up in my chair every day for as long as I could stand it, so Mom would time it a little longer each day. For the first six months after surgery, I wasn't allowed to try to bend or twist, or do any crawling. Nowadays, I still can't bend or twist very far, because of the rods in my back. Before the rods were inserted, if I dropped something down by my feet, I could bend down and get it. Now, I can only reach to my knees.

I really wanted to start feeling better in my wheelchair so that I could play the piano more. Sometimes I'd tell my parents my back didn't hurt too much, even if it did, so that they'd let me play a little longer. After a while, the pain started to ease up, which, thankfully, meant more music time. For weeks, I still didn't have much of an appetite; then one day, Granddaddy brought me an apple fritter and I ate the whole thing. From then on, my appetite was back to normal—the power of dessert. Mom was so glad she fed me as if each meal was going to be my last.

After being cooped up in the house for months, my doctor said I could go outside soon. "Mom, can I get on the swing? Please?" I begged. I loved the feeling of flying through the air.

Finally, she agreed. I couldn't wait to get out there. Granddaddy wheeled me out into the backyard, and he and Mom picked me up and moved me to our swing. I held on while he pushed me—swinging was just as much fun as I'd remembered. Not wanting me to overdo it, Mom soon told me it was time to go back inside for lunch. I begged Granddaddy for just one more push, and he agreed. One last, big push and . . .

Creeaak! The chain on one side of the swing snapped. In an instant, I fell to the ground and started rolling down the driveway before anyone could stop me.

The grownups screamed and came running. Quickly, they examined me and carried me straight to the van. My back didn't seem to hurt any more than usual, but Mom and Granddaddy worried that the fall might have messed up the rods. They wanted to get X-rays to make sure everything was okay. On the way to the hospital, I realized my leg was throbbing and starting to swell. Granddaddy's voice sounded strained, and he kept apologizing and asking me if I was all right. I told him I was okay; a little pain never hurt anybody. But my leg was getting worse, and when Mom touched it, it hurt pretty bad. At the hospital, we found out my back was fine. But my leg was broken.

Now Granddaddy felt even worse, saying he'd never forgive himself. "I should have checked the chains before I let him on the swing. If I did, this wouldn't have happened," he kept saying. But I told him it wasn't his fault and hugged him. The chains were rusty and it just happened—it could have happened to anyone.

Of course, I had to get this big-old cast on my leg, which put me back to square one in my recovery. But this time, the pain wasn't nearly as bad as it was after my back operation. I guess you could say the back operation prepared me for anything that might come along. Mom would say that's one of those hidden blessings. The not-so-blessed part was I couldn't go swimming for another eight weeks. I love to swim because I feel so light in the water. Even though I can't walk on land, in water I can stand and do a sort-of walk on the bottom. Dad would take Jesse and Cameron to the pool, but they had to leave me behind. I didn't like that one bit, but knew that's just the way it had to be. Anyway, those weeks really weren't so bad, because I could still play the piano. And in time, Granddaddy finally forgave himself when he saw I was doing just fine.

DAD

How did we cope? Sometimes, it's not easy, especially when you think a challenge is over, and then there it is again, staring you in the face, like the need for more surgeries. Maybe it's knowing your son is in pain and there's nothing you can do about it, or knowing he will never see anything in his life, never walk or stand on his own.

We thought that was the extent of it—his blindness and inability to walk or stand—until the doctors tried to straighten Patrick Henry's arms and felt the resistance. He was still a baby, and at first, they thought it was just a muscle problem, a reflex they could work through with therapy and get the muscles to relax. But soon it became apparent that the problem was structural. We learned that Patrick Henry had a condition called pterygium syndrome—the knees and elbows are in a constant state of contracture. The way Patrick Henry's joints and muscles were formed couldn't be fixed. On top of everything else, he'd never be able to extend his arms.

So just when you think you've got the big challenges under control, something else crops up to prevent your complete sigh of relief. Maybe it's thinking you've lost your son forever, that anesthesia had made him retreat to a world we could no longer share. Maybe it's an unkind comment from people who don't have a clue what you're going through, or surly professionals talking down to you. Or maybe it's never knowing for certain if you are doing enough, or if what you are doing is the right thing. All these things make coping anything but easy. But you have to always commit to moving ahead, with the belief that things won't get better without your doing everything possible to make it so.

And even when you feel as though you are facing it all alone, you have to believe you're not. God is there, waiting for an invitation to intercede. It may not come when you think it should or in the form you had requested, but exactly what is needed always arrives at exactly the right time.

Do All You Can to Change What You Can

PATRICK HENRY

Some things in life can improve and some things can't. With me, it was obvious that many things weren't going to get any better than they were—I'd never be able to see, for example. But other things might improve, and I learned at a young age that the only way to achieve change was if we rolled up our sleeves and did everything we could, and this included many surgeries and different kinds of therapy.

I've learned that when situations are challenging, you have to rise up and keep going, or they'll get you down and keep you there. I'd remind myself of this when I'd try to get around our house on my own in my wheelchair and encounter obstacles—from narrow doorways tough to squeeze through to furniture in my path.

Or when my brother, Jesse, and I were younger, we'd have races. I could have said, "I can't race, Jesse," and decided not to compete, because he's strong and fast—everything I'm not. But I *could* race in some ways, like seeing who could open the van door first, or get off the bed and onto the floor fastest, and it turned out that sometimes I'd even win, but to know that I had to try.

Each semester, I can't get the audio software I need for my textbooks in college until we're well into the term. This is frustrating, and I could say that I can't do the work and quit. But that would defeat my goal of an education.

As I've met so many people, I've noticed that everyone eventually faces some kind of major challenge in his or her life. But I've also noticed that with problems big or small, it can be tough to get out of your comfort zone to take them on. Usually, it's fear of failure or of another kind of pain. If you give in to that fear, you might never know how good things could be. Or, the problem might get even worse if you choose to ignore it. That was the case with my scoliosis and with the fitting of my prosthetic eyes.

When it came to trying to improve my physical disabilities, Mom and Dad would never give up, so we kept pushing. Anytime I felt afraid—whether it was going back for another fitting of braces, another surgery, a more painful therapy—the hope I had for a better life helped me endure the worst. I knew I had to keep trying, no matter what, and now, I wouldn't have it any other way.

Chapter 3

Pursue Your Passion
as If Your Life Depends on It

There is only one passion, the passion for happiness.
—DENIS DIDEROT

PATRICK HENRY

When I play music, especially classical pieces, everything changes. I feel the music moving through me. It surrounds me, lifting me, like I'm swimming in water and feeling lighter. When I play Debussy's *Clair de Lune* (which means "light of the moon" in French), even though I don't know what moonlight looks like, I think about a beautiful night outside with a soft breeze blowing. And as I keep playing, I'm there, experiencing it.

All my life, all I've ever wanted to do was play music. Piano was my first love. I've always been a pretty laid-back guy, and as a kid, about the only times I can remember getting mad were when piano time was cut short for some reason.

49

I know that for some kids, music lessons are kind of forced on them. Lots of people I meet tell me that their parents made them practice the piano or some other musical instrument. "I used to count the minutes until practice time was over!" "Oh, I hated the lessons I had to take even more," they'll say. That always makes me laugh, because practicing has never been a chore to me, only a pleasure. Music is my key to life. The more I play, the richer my life becomes.

I'm often asked if I missed not being able to go out and do most activities other kids can do, like play sports. I haven't experienced it, so I don't miss it. My brother Jesse is a great athlete, a star in baseball and football. When he practices, it's not work; it's play. We all have our own skills and talents to share, and each of us should be proud of what we can do, because we all can be good at something. Most important is that you genuinely love what you are doing.

People always want to know how I got started playing the piano. I guess you could say it was more by accident than anything intentional. Actually, it was Dad who got me going.

It all goes back to the first time Mom left me alone with Dad when I was a baby. At first he was sure he could handle it. His plan (Dad always has a plan) was to get me to bed, and then he'd catch a ball game on TV. Just as Mom always did, Dad fed me, changed me, and had me in my pajamas, figuring he was right on schedule. I should be happy, right? Full belly, clean diaper.

But, no. I started screaming at the top of my lungs. Dad had never really dealt with this before, because Mom was always the one to calm me down, and everything would go like clockwork. He was just a new dad and didn't quite know how to handle a screaming baby, so he tried everything he thought Mom would do. He gave me more formula from my bottle, but I didn't want it. He checked my diaper; no problem there. He bounced me up and down on his knee. He hummed, then sang to me. He moved to the rocking chair and rocked me. Nothing worked.

Dad walked me across the floor, back and forth, back and forth, first slowly, then faster. I was still screaming. At this point, he decided just to put me in my crib. For a moment, I quieted. Then he closed the door, and I started wailing even louder. Dad was fed up by now, and I can't blame him.

He didn't come back at my first cries. This was a test of wills, he figured. Surely, eventually, I'd exhaust myself and fall asleep. But Dad soon started feeling guilty. What if all that hard crying did something bad, like rupture a blood vessel or harm my vocal cords? He held out another minute, standing by the nursery door while he thought I was running out of steam, but I was just regrouping. "Okay, you win," he grumbled, taking me out of my crib. Time to repeat the routine: bouncing, humming, singing, rocking, walking.

Dad is not really a patient man, and back then, he was even less patient than he is now. I was getting on his last nerve. But he says when he looked at my puffy, red face, even though his head was splitting, he felt nothing but deep love for me. Then he walked me some more.

With all my crying, Dad gave up trying to watch his baseball game on TV. He wished Mom was there, but he didn't dare call her, knowing he'd never hear the end of it. He could just hear her voice: "I leave you alone with our son once in a blue moon, and you call me in less than an hour to come home and rescue you . . . and for what, so you can watch one of your stupid ball games?"

By this time, Dad was counting the minutes until Mom was supposed to be home. He just sat with me on his knee and stared at me, wondering how I could keep it up. At that moment, he glanced over at the piano.

He stood up, walked over to the piano, and laid my blanket on top of it. Our piano is a high upright that sits against the wall in the family room. The piano is narrow on top, and he put me right there, laying me on my back on the blanket. Dad now admits this was probably pretty precarious, if not downright dangerous. He was sure if Mom had seen him do this, she would have wrung his neck.

He moved me closer to the wall, and I seemed stable, but I was still screaming bloody murder. Now what? My dad is a musician himself—he loves to take requests—so he sat quickly and started softly playing a lullaby. Boom! I stopped crying, immediately. Dad was amazed. I was so quiet, he checked to make sure I was still breathing. I was. He said a quick thank you prayer and started playing again, this time something more upbeat. It was a miracle! The angels in heaven were probably looking down at him and laughing out loud, saying, "I knew that thick-headed young man would figure it out sooner or later."

Dad continued serenading me as I lay there on top of the piano, still and quiet. At one point, he stopped and I started squirming a little, so he continued. It didn't seem to matter what the music was, as long as he was playing. Why did the piano quiet me when nothing else could? Since that day, we've never been able to answer the question. Maybe it was the vibrations against my body that soothed me. Perhaps it was the sound itself, something new and magical to me. Or was it something simpler, like I was just scared to death? I guess we'll never know.

DAD

From that point on, whenever I was pressed into babysitting duty, the piano thing worked like a charm. Many years later, reflecting on this, I thought about how playing the piano had come so naturally to me as well, even at a young age. Back then, entertaining was a way to put myself in the spotlight and attract the recognition I craved. Now I realize it meant something more—preparation to help me raise a special child, a child who would be limited in many ways except when it comes to music.

If I hadn't been a piano player, would Patrick Henry ever have discovered his unique talents? Who knows? Thankfully, the answer doesn't matter. But I've had the recurring thought that God sent Patrick Henry specifically to us, that his birth was much more than just the accidental joining of two infinitely rare recessive genes. If so, it was the perfect match. I could expose him to the piano very early in life, and my son could teach me to grow up.

PATRICK HENRY

At about the age of nine months, I was able to sit up on my own, so Dad decided to put me in an old wooden highchair and sit me at the piano to see what I might do. He figured that I'd probably enjoy pounding on the keys.

As Dad anticipated, I absolutely loved it. But I never banged on the keys. Dad says I struck them gently and respectfully, as if they were fragile and might break. He let me play with the keys as long as I wanted, surprised I didn't get bored quickly. Just the opposite: With each note, I was fascinated.

Once I got started, every day afterward, I had to have some kind of piano time. The earliest memories I have at the piano are how the various notes would remind me of voices. Some notes made me think of my parents or grandparents, and some reminded me of the voice of a child. Others reminded me of a male or female voice I had heard in public.

One day, Dad hit a key. I listened to the sound, then found the exact note and played it back to him. Dad was astounded. Probably a lucky guess, an accident, he thought, especially since I couldn't see the keyboard, nor extend my arms and reach very easily. So Dad did it again, and not only was I able to find the exact key, according to Dad, I struck it like a maestro. He did it again, and I responded correctly. We went on like that for a while, and I didn't want to quit. When repeating a note didn't seem to be much of a challenge, Dad started playing three random notes from different areas of the keyboard. I would play them back.

How was I able to do that? A lot of people have asked me that over the years. It just seemed natural, like the way other toddlers take their first steps. How did they know how to balance, stand upright, and put one foot in front of the other? They just can because it feels right.

Dad likes to have answers to things and he tried to figure it out. He told me he sat there, closed his eyes, and imagined he was a youngster still in diapers. How would he find the exact notes on a piano in the right sequence without ever having seen someone else do it first? And even then, how could he remember where the keys were? He knew that when I struck the keys, I wasn't just fooling around, but playing them deliberately. At nine months old, I'd be in deep thought, concentrating on the tones. Dad figures I was developing an understanding of some sort of spacing relationship, so that when I heard a certain key, I knew it was to my left, or my right, and approximately how far away it was. Maybe so.

My parents were also amazed I could count back then. Not only could I locate the keys, but I could also hit them a precise number of times. I could do this if Dad struck the same note once, twice, or three or four times in a row, or if he struck several keys at random.

I really enjoyed this seek-and-find game, and I'd light up each time I was successful. Dad couldn't understand this, either—how I seemed to know without him telling me or cheering. I just knew I had played exactly the right notes. After a while, I think Dad gave up trying to figure it all out and just accepted that God had given me a wonderful gift.

DAD

I loved it, especially that we were doing this activity together. I couldn't have imagined it, but here I was, enjoying something so satisfying with my son, our baby, who had so much going against him and would never be considered normal. Normal? Thank you, God, that my son is anything *but* normal!

Everything about his talent was amazing, so I guess I shouldn't have been surprised that Patrick Henry quickly learned to play rhythms back to me. Was there a limit to what he could play by ear, and at such a young age? I decided to find out. Each day, the listening and playing exercises increased and became more challenging. This went on for months, and before he was two years old, we were playing melodies and harmonies together. Patrick Henry would accompany me on the piano while I played violin. I would put his cassette player by the piano, and he would play along with his *Sesame Street* recordings.

I loved showing him off when we had company. I'd ask him to play "Twinkle, Twinkle Little Star" or "You Are My

Sunshine," and he'd do it perfectly. My chest would swell to the breaking point, although it shouldn't have. It wasn't me doing all this great stuff, and I wasn't such a wonderful teacher that I was able to create this two-year-old protégé. All I did was expose him to the piano and teach him some rudimentary things. From there, it was all Patrick Henry's doing.

Nowadays, after Patrick Henry plays piano for an audience, they are, of course, astounded at his ability to play and sing from many different genres—classical selections, contemporary music, country and western, you name it. I worry that many of those listening may think of me as a musician parent who has a blind child and who had it in his mind to create the next Ray Charles, Stevie Wonder, or Ronnie Milsap. Actually, it was just the opposite.

My son could entertain himself for hours at the piano while my wife and I cleaned the house or worked in the yard. We had monitors so we could hear him inside the house playing merrily if we were outside. He never once stopped, took a break, or wondered where we were. When Patrick Henry played, he was in another world.

In fact, it became a challenge to get him away from the piano. As a child, he was very demanding. Often, he was dissatisfied just to play piano on his own and insisted I play along with him. I think at some deep level, he knew I craved it and got as much out of our sessions as he did. This was our baseball pitch and catch, a father and son enjoying each other. We would never play football, go golfing, or do any of the sports I had longed for, but that was okay, because God had another plan, a bigger and better version of anything I could have imagined. This, I believe, was why I could play violin, piano, guitar, and trumpet and was a music major in college. It was all in preparation for the most important role I would play in my life.

And so the piano became a way of life. Patrick Henry never missed a day, unless we were away at someplace that had no instrument. Even then, it was likely he'd have his toy keyboard with him.

PATRICK HENRY

I remember my basket of toys. It contained mostly toys that made some sort of noise—squeaks and bells were my favorite. I would squeeze them and roll them around, wanting to hear the sounds. I loved cassette tapes, too. Every night before I went to bed, I would have to listen to one. Two of my favorites were a version of "Peter and the Wolf," a story about a boy who caught a wolf in the forest and took him to the zoo. I also enjoyed a tape known as "The Orchestra," where a man talked about the various types of ensembles (chamber, symphony, philharmonic), what music can represent, how music is written, and the different instruments that make up each orchestral section.

Kind of funny that a little kid would enjoy hearing about piccolos and percussion, but I was obsessed. Other little kids love children's songs, so why would it be so unusual if I liked the orchestra? Same thing, sort of, isn't it? I guess I felt I was more like other kids than different from them. I know I wanted to feel that way.

Every day, Dad would teach me new musical notes and chords. I would play a note, and Dad would either sing it or tell me the note was an F-sharp or an E-flat, or whatever the case may be. I would play a set of two notes, after which Dad would tell me those two notes were a perfect fourth, or a major third, or minor second or an octave. At that age, I couldn't tell my dad in certain words that I wanted to know how a piano worked, but he knew I did. Above the keyboard of our old upright piano was a pair of doors, which you could open to expose the hammers. Dad opened the doors, took my hands, and had me feel a hammer strike the wire string and make it vibrate as I hit a key. I wanted to feel the vibration of every single string. This is how I learned to play, and each time I learned something, I wanted to know more. I guess you could say I was addicted to the piano.

After I'd learned a few simple songs, Dad and I played another game. I would sit in my high chair and play the melody, and Dad would sit at the other end of the piano and create an accompaniment. Playing piano with my father was so much fun I always wanted him to be there. It wasn't just the music; it was sharing something we both loved. But Dad had a job and other commitments, so I had to accept that he couldn't always be around when I wanted to play. I didn't like it, but you can't always have things just the way you want them.

When I started going to elementary school, each day before I left for school, I had to make sure I had enough piano time to be able to accompany a whole nursery rhyme tape from front to back. If I had to stop before the tape was done, I'd get upset and would threaten to write angry notes complaining to my teachers. Thinking about that now, it must have been funny to my parents—"I'm going to tell on you to my teachers!"

Dad was my piano teacher until I was about five. He was great, so patient with me, and he made it fun. At that point, he decided I needed a "real" teacher to take over, someone who could help me move to another level. My second teacher was Miss Deanna Scoggins. She was also blind, and when Dad refers back to that time, he calls it "the blind leading the blind." He means that as a sincere compliment, because he really wanted Miss Deanna to be my teacher and was glad when she accepted.

Dad never taught me proper finger technique for the piano—how to set your hands and which fingers to use for which notes. I just did what came naturally as I went along, and that seemed to work. I don't have much flexibility in my hands and fingers. I can't hold a spoon or a pencil the way most people do, and can't do a lot of things with my hands—things most people take for granted. This complicates my playing, because in addition to the limitations imposed by my fingers and hands, I can't extend my arms and my reach is limited. So my approach is somewhat eclectic.

When Dad was a kid, although he loved playing the piano, the one thing he hated was having to learn technique. The browbeating he got from his teacher was such agony that he resisted as much as he could. Dad was worried that a sighted teacher would see my ragtag approach and want to correct it, taking me all the way back to square one. But mostly he didn't want anyone to take the fun out of my playing.

Miss Deanna couldn't see how I maybe didn't use my pinky finger exactly as I should, or curve my hand correctly, or other ways I violated proper ways of doing things. Because she was blind, my technique was never an issue, and I could just focus on the music itself. This made her the perfect teacher for me. We'd concentrate on what I call the "short classics," Bach minuets or Beethoven sonatinas, by following the standard Suzuki method of teaching—listen and imitate. It's similar to the way kids learn a language.

Miss Deanna worked with me for five years, right up to my last surgery for scoliosis at age ten. After the surgery, I needed to take a break for quite a while, because I couldn't sit up to play, and when I could sit up, it was difficult to sit for long periods. Without the piano, it was like a piece of my life had been stolen. My family would tell me, "It'll pass, just hang on," and it did, but it seemed like forever.

Finally, when my back improved, I was able to return to the keyboard, and it was as if I hadn't missed a day. Everyone was surprised that I could remember all I did and still play the way I used to. For me, it was like picking fruit. I couldn't reach it for a long time, but when I came back to the tree, there was the fruit, hanging low and waiting for me.

By that point, Miss Deanna had told my parents she had taken me as far as she could and they should find me a more accomplished teacher. "Someday, he'll be really good if he keeps working hard," she said. When Dad told me this, I laughed, as if I was ever going to quit for any reason. At my last lesson, Dad and I thanked her for all she had done for me, and she gave me a kiss good-bye on my cheek.

Sometimes folks wonder why you still need a music teacher once you've come so far and can play well. Without one, you can't learn the skills to take on more challenging pieces. After I stopped taking lessons with Miss Deanna, I started to get bored, because I kept playing the same things over and over. When I performed in public, I often played a classical selection. But when I was on my own, I really enjoyed lullabies. I'd sing along, too, and since my voice was still soft and high-pitched, like the Vienna Boys' Choir, sometimes I'd put Mom and Dad to sleep.

Maybe he just couldn't listen to any more Brahms, but Dad stepped up his efforts to locate someone for me. The next teacher he found had impeccable credentials, exactly what he was looking for, and so my new lessons began. But things didn't go so well.

As feared, this new teacher was appalled at my technique and set about correcting all my bad habits. He was the expert, so if he decided I needed to make all these changes to be a better musician, so be it. But my attempts were awkward, and I have to say, it wasn't as much fun as working with Miss Deanna.

Dad saw what was going on and tried to intervene, to plead my case. He assumed this guy would understand that I loved playing the piano and that's why I played. Dad didn't hire him to make me into the next Liberace or Van Cliburn. But my father couldn't convince him. In fact, after a few lessons, the teacher told my parents the only way he'd continue is if Dad butted out and didn't attend my lessons. Well, you can imagine how Dad responded. He was furious, and that ended that.

Finding someone new wasn't easy, and the search dragged on. Then, as always when it's most important, exactly the right thing happened.

Once, when I was younger, maybe about eight, Dad had taken me to a local piano store to try out some of the better instruments. I got to play on one of the big pianos, a baby grand—what a treat. What we didn't know was that when I was there, an accomplished Juilliard-trained piano teacher, Miss Hinda Ordman, was listening while I played Bach's Minuet in G-major. She says that when she heard me, she was awestruck and told someone there at the store that she'd love to have me as a student.

Years later, when Dad was trying to find a new teacher for me, we went to the piano store to see if we could get a recommendation. While Dad was talking to the owner, Miss Hinda walked out of the studio and recognized us. She was on her way out of the store, but stopped to talk to us and overheard that we were looking for a teacher. Thrilled, she agreed to take me on as a pupil on the spot. Dad took her aside and talked to her about my physical limitations when it came to performing and learning perfect technique. Would that be a problem? She understood right away, and more than anything, she didn't want to take the fun out of my playing. We sealed the deal, and I took lessons at the store with her for the next three years.

When Miss Hinda started working with me, I was about twelve and playing at about an intermediate level. I didn't like reading music by Braille, even though I could, so for my lessons, Miss Hinda would record the piece we were working on and she'd play it very slowly to make sure I could hear every single note. She had to do a ton of work before I even showed up for my lesson. But she says she didn't mind, because I was always so enthusiastic.

When she teaches her sighted students at this level, she makes them play with the fallboard down, blocking their view of the keys. When you are always searching for the keys with your eyes, you bob your head up and down, looking up at the music, then down at the keys. At first, students don't like doing this, because it's such a change from what they are used to. She told me, "See how lucky you are, I don't have to do that with you."

There are eighty-eight keys on the keyboard, and I wish I could hit them all. If you ever see me play, you'll see that my elbows are close to my sides. That doesn't make sense for playing a wide instrument, especially when you have to go to the extreme ends of the keyboard. But that's the way my arms are. So, when I'm practicing challenging pieces by Mendelssohn or other greats, I might have to lean my body as far as I can and use my right hand to "cheat" a little bit when I'm supposed to be using only my left. Or sometimes I'm supposed to play a chord with five notes, but I can hit only three. The music won't be as rich as it should be, but

Miss Hinda would tell me to do what I needed to make it work. I love that about her, her flexibility. Even though she was trained in the classical tradition at Juilliard, the way of the masters, her attitude is a lot like Dad's—let's do what we have to do to get it done.

Miss Hinda told Dad she'd never had a student like me. We assumed that, of course, she meant a student without eyes and limitations in using his arms. No, she meant that no matter what she threw at me, I was eager to take it on. She'd give me an assignment she expected to take a long time to master, but I'd be back the next week, ready for the next step. Once she asked me, "Patrick Henry, when you're not here, don't you ever sleep?" I told her I practice every chance I get, which, when I thought about it, was day and night. I told her I sleep, too, but not too much.

Eventually, the piano store closed and we moved my lessons to Miss Hinda's house. There was always something pleasant to smell, to breathe in and hold. Sometimes, it was freshly baked chocolate chip cookies, or the sweetness of flowers, or a fragrant perfume. I'd try to figure out what it was when I first came in the door. It was so warm there, so welcoming. It was like I was home.

DAD

There was an instant bonding between my son and Hinda Ordman. On day one, Patrick Henry said, "May I kiss you?" She agreed with great enthusiasm, and from then on, their lessons always start with a hug and kiss on the cheek, and end the same way. Patrick Henry is accustomed to getting his way with the ladies, but one time at Hinda's, he experienced his first rejection.

We were coming in for a lesson, and one of Hinda's female students was just finishing up. She was Patrick Henry's age, about fifteen. They were introduced, and then my son popped the question. "May I give you a kiss?" She paused a moment, a little flustered, then said, "No, thank you." I watched Patrick Henry's face. He looked as if he had been handed a rubber snake and didn't know what to do with it. He said, "Oh . . . okay." Then she came over to him and shook his hand. I told him later it was a consolation prize. I also told him that his success rate with the fairer sex was running about 99 percent, much better than any other male in the history of the world, including Warren Beatty and Don Juan, so he shouldn't fret too much about that encounter.

I usually would drop Patrick Henry off, run some errands, then return to pick him up. Sometimes, when I'd return a bit early, I'd walk in on the tail end of the tape Hinda had prepared for his lesson. There was always what she called "a little love message," like "Have a wonderful week. You are the greatest, the apple of my eye." Or, "You are my chocolate chip cookie." He'd listen and smile really big, then he'd return the sentiments. He likes to call her his little matzo ball, reflecting her Jewish heritage. She says that when we are traveling and he has to skip a lesson and she doesn't see him for a week, she misses him. I believe her.

Hinda once told me about a conversation she had with

Patrick Henry during a lesson. "Your son has amazed me many times and on many levels, but this time took the prize," she said. They were chatting as they usually do between efforts, and she had asked him, did he ever wish to be able to see some of the things he'd never seen? And since they had known each other quite a while, would he want to know what she looked like? She was surprised at Patrick Henry's quick response. "I already know what you look like," he said. "You are kind and generous, beautiful in every way."

I think the litmus test for passion is how you react when your love is taken from you. There was a time when Patrick Henry could not play the piano because of his back operation. He accepted not being able to play under those conditions, knowing he'd get back to it as soon as he was able. But when he cannot play because of our tight traveling schedule, he experiences real withdrawal. Most people wouldn't notice his subtle change in mood. For example, if I mention that I see a beautiful piano in a store, mall, or hotel lobby, he'll want me to take him to it right away. If there isn't time, he's fine, but I can tell he's a little wistful.

PATRICK HENRY

In 2001, we took a family vacation to a Tennessee resort. We were away almost a week, and we had fun. But five days without my piano is like forever, and I was starting to have severe piano withdrawal. Dad knew I was feeling down, even though I tried to hide it.

While there, we went to church to attend Mass, and afterward, Dad asked the choir director if I could play the piano a little bit before they locked up. Later, he told me the man gave him a funny look, because I guess it was a strange request. And seeing my condition, maybe he worried I'd just pound on the piano and do some damage. But the director agreed.

I wanted to play about six different pieces all at the same time. I settled on Beethoven's *Moonlight Sonata*. The folks in the foyer who were leaving stopped at the door and came back in to listen. They gathered around the piano, and just like that, we had a little unexpected classical music recital.

Dad teases me that I'm a ham, and I guess I am. But, honestly, I don't want to play to attract attention. If people are quiet, I don't even know or notice that they're around me. I just love to play.

Today, Mr. Pete Pino, the choir director of that church, and his wife, Bonnie, are our friends and two of our favorite people. Since our first visit, we've gone back to that same resort several times. On the first return trip, we gave a concert for everyone in town. And after that, Dad and I were invited back to give talks and perform at a number of functions. The piano has become more than a passion; it's my way of connecting with folks who are strangers.

Lessons at Miss Hinda's were going fine and continued into my teens, but a problem eventually cropped up. There are steep steps leading up to her front door, and as I got heavier, it was harder for Dad to carry me. He worried he might drop me if he slipped. He hated to do it and delayed as long as he could, but eventually he had to tell her he couldn't bring me anymore. We knew I'd be going to the University of Louisville soon, and we hoped I could pick up my lessons again there.

But Miss Hinda wouldn't hear of it. She's so cool, she just said, "That's fine. Then I'll come to your house." Dad told her he'd pay her extra to cover her inconvenience, but she said no, and she's been coming to our house ever since. We all see her as part of our extended family. She's like a second mother to me.

Thank goodness she did agree to continue with me, because we soon found out that because I'm not majoring in music at the University of Louisville, none of the piano professors would be able to take me on as a student. But as always, things turned out perfectly, as Dr. Michael Tunnell agreed to work with me on the trumpet. So, with Miss Hinda and Dr. Tunnell at U of L, I'm blessed with two of the best teachers in the world.

Most folks assume I would be a music major in college, but I'm not. I've fallen in love with something else, too—the Spanish language. From the first time I heard it spoken, I wanted to learn as much about it as I could, so I'm majoring in Spanish. Dad told me that whether or not I majored in music wouldn't matter so much in the real world. For example, at an orchestra tryout, the people who evaluate you don't care about the degree. You actually audition behind a curtain, so they don't know who you are or what you look like. All you have to do is play extremely well.

DAD

Sometimes it feels as if your passion has dried up and disappeared, when life seems to be just another day: up in the morning, stumbling through the routine, then falling into bed at night. Among the many things I admire about my son is the genuine excitement and dedication he brings to everything he pursues, and not just his music. The great leaders of our time tell us the common denominator among the truly successful is a strong drive to pursue what makes life worthwhile, whatever that might be.

At twenty, Patrick Henry still has a childlike enthusiasm for life, and I think that's another thing that sets him apart. By childlike, I don't mean childish. I mean the passion we are born with and display when very young, doing something because we love it and for no other reason. Watch children run around the playground. They aren't running to get fit or lose weight or prepare for an upcoming race; they run because it's fun. That's the way Patrick Henry approaches everything he does.

How has he held on to his childlike passion, especially in the face of all he has been through, all he has endured? One thought I've had is that Patrick Henry has never had the luxury of a lot of discretionary time. The tasks he performs in everyday life—things the rest of us take for granted and can do quickly, like washing up or putting on shoes—are laborious and time-consuming for him. And when he isn't being assisted, he is literally spinning his wheels waiting for help, waiting for something to be done. So when he finally has the opportunity to engage in things he enjoys, like playing the piano, it's special and he is intent on maximizing every single moment.

My son has rekindled my passion for life. He has shown me how important family is and how we are like a team, bonded at a deep level. And as many coaches say, there is no *I* in *team*. I love that we have the opportunity to make regular public appearances, and I love traveling with my son. Usually, Patrick Henry and I give a little talk, and then he performs. I look forward to every appearance, no matter where it is, how hard it is to get there, how long it takes, how little sleep I've had the night before, or how many folks are likely to show up. It's become the childlike passion of mine, pumping new life into my existence. Finally, I have a purpose in life that is bigger than me: teaming with my son to spread God's message of possibilities and unconditional love to all who choose to listen. It's wonderful, and I owe it all to Patrick Henry.

Pursue Your Passion
as If Your Life Depends on It

PATRICK HENRY

Sounds bring my world to life. Whether it's church bells, horns, sirens, heels clicking on pavement, voice tones, the jingle of a cell phone, laughter, applause, the hum of a lawn mower—they all tell me a story. Sounds are my primary source of pleasure, amusement, and information, which is why the piano may be more important to me than it is to others.

More than that, music is the ultimate challenge. The most exciting life pursuits are the ones you can never fully master. I thought I was getting close to learning all I could about the piano until I met Miss Hinda. I might have been close to the top of a little hill, but she showed me that when I got there, I'd find another mountain range up ahead waiting for me. The challenge it brings is what gets me through every day.

Do what you love, and love what you do; that's the secret to success. My dad didn't have the opportunity to do that for much of his life, especially as an adult, often having to settle for doing what was necessary. I think that's why he's so supportive of me, helping me pursue my dreams and, now that I'm in college, encouraging me to pursue Spanish just because I love it. I have other responsibilities now and don't have as much time for music as I'd like, but I still spend as much time as I can with it because when I'm playing—or looking forward to it—I'm the happiest. Some of us haven't found that thing in life that swallows us and fulfills us like nothing else can. All you have to do is keep trying new things. You'll find it, and when you do, you'll realize it's what you've been looking for all your life. I'm blessed to have discovered the piano when I was very young, but you can discover new passions, no matter what your age. I believe everyone needs something precious, something that makes a person want to get out of bed every morning and get to it immediately.

Someone once asked me if I thought of a passion as an escape. "For me," she said, "my music helps me get away from my job." Thinking about her words, I couldn't come up with anything I'd be escaping from. But then I realized that maybe music is an escape. It's an escape to places inside me that I can't reach any other way.

Chapter 4

Be the *You* Your Mother Would Be Proud Of

My mother had a great deal of trouble with me, but I think she enjoyed it.

— MARK TWAIN

PATRICK HENRY

When did I first realize I was different from other people? My first inkling came very early on in life, probably when I was no more than a toddler.

People liked to hold me, and I would explore them with my hands. I noticed that their eyes were soft and fluttered to the touch. My eyes were hard and stayed still, no matter what. But then I'd do things like touch my Dad's beard, which felt fuzzy, coarse, and very different from my soft facial skin—yet different from my brothers' faces, too. And certainly, Mom and Dad treated me like anyone else. So I just figured that adults were different from children, and each of us was unique.

75

At the time, I assumed everyone struggled to stand—that like me, people couldn't do it on their own—and that nobody could walk. I'm not sure I really even understood then what walking was. When you're blind and really young, your world is tiny and you have a tough time thinking about life outside yourself. But as I got a little older, I probably began to wonder how others were able to pick me up and carry me, or get things for me. They must be able to do something I can't do. Gradually, I came to realize I was *more* different from others and had "special needs," because I couldn't walk. And when I did realize this, I made up my mind to do everything I could to be less different.

I had to first find a way to stand up on my own. I was able to stand for short periods if Mom or Dad leaned me against something, like the coffee table. My knees are like my elbows; they don't extend. Since my knees are always flexed I'm always in a semi-sitting position, so if I wasn't supported, I'd fall over backwards.

Standing on my own was my goal, but no matter how hard I tried, I couldn't get it done. Then I discovered I could do better when I had my hip and leg braces on. The braces had a heavy metal base and a stand that supported me from behind while the braces stretched my knee joints, trying to straighten them. Dad now compares these to the medieval torture rack, where someone turned a crank and stretched your body. The braces were uncomfortable, and my parents didn't want to put them on me too often, because they didn't seem to really help straightening my body. (Because I don't have hip joints, the hip braces couldn't make those joints work better; nor did the leg braces seem to have any lasting effects on my knees.) But I didn't mind wearing them so much when I found they gave me enough support that I could stand by myself.

Mom says I thought this was pretty cool ("Hey, look at me!"). But the truth is, the base and the stand were just like the coffee table, something to keep me from falling backward. When I figured this out, I wasn't so anxious to put my braces on anymore. Today, I still can't stand on my own without some kind of support.

The big breakthrough came when I was about four years old and got my wheelchair. Some folks might think I would have felt terrible that I'd be living my life in that chair. Not me, though. I loved it. I could now move around like everyone else, plus I'd get a nice ride that others didn't have. But I developed a bad habit. I liked to put my hands on the wheels to feel them spin as I moved, the rubber flicking against my skin. "Don't ever do that, Patrick Henry," Mom would warn me, but I did it anyway. What harm could it do? One day, a babysitter pushed me really fast in a race against Jesse, who was about two years old. We won, but I got bad brush-burns on my hands. Ouch! They hurt like crazy and needed to be bandaged. From then on, I knew why I wasn't supposed to stick my hands on the wheels.

There were a few times when I asked my parents, "Why can't I walk like everyone else?" I wasn't upset, but I was curious.

"God made us all different, and that's how he made you," Mom would say. They'd also tell me that although others can walk, they can't play the piano like me. It was as if God had a big box of abilities and he pulled things out and gave them to you when you were born.

I accepted their explanation, which seemed perfectly reasonable. But when I say things like, "Okay, I can't walk, no big deal," I've learned that sometimes, this can be confusing or misinterpreted. Some might think I don't care or that I'm hiding from reality. I do care, very much. If God said to me, "Patrick Henry, would you like to start walking today?" I'd immediately say yes. I believe most people in a wheelchair would love to be independent of their chair and live life completely on their own. But nothing is accomplished by dwelling on the fact you can't walk. So you have to shrink its importance in your mind, reduce it from a big deal to a small deal, and that's what I've done.

But more than that, I look for the trade-offs God gives us, like my ability to play the piano. There's another benefit I wouldn't want to give up. I love to touch others and be touched, to be held and to cuddle. The fact that I can't walk, especially when I was young, gave everyone an excuse to always be touching me for one reason or the other. To me, that's a big deal.

At a young age, I knew that adults are the ones who would lift and carry me, hug me, and not mind if I touched them. They were also the ones who fed me, and you know how much I love to eat. Other kids my age couldn't care less about what I might need, and if I couldn't keep up with them, too bad, off they went. So I quickly decided that in my world, adults were my choice for companionship. But since I was always spending time with adults, my granny got worried that I wouldn't know how to interact with my peers. She told Mom I needed to be in a day-care center.

Mom wasn't too keen on the idea. She had gone down that road before, trying to find a good place for me, but without any success. No one, it seemed, wanted to take on a blind, disabled kid. This time, however, she got lucky. The Wesley Community House said it would take me in its day-care program, no problem. I was a toddler at the time.

That first day, Mom took me to the center and dropped me off. Or rather, she tried to—she said the staff practically had to carry her back to her car to get her out of there. She cried all the way to work, anxious all day long that something horrible might happen. She needn't have worried; I had a wonderful time. The purpose of my going, I know, was to get me involved with other kids, but it didn't quite work out that way at first. In the morning, Miss Naomi and Miss Geraldine served breakfast, then took turns hovering over me until lunch. Then Miss Rita and Miss Lois came in, served lunch, and did the same. There also was Miss Betty, Miss Ruby, Ms. Garvin, and Miss Bess, plus Miss Arnetta, the director. At five o'clock, just before Mom came back, Miss Rita and I had cuddle time. It was great, and I couldn't wait to go back the next day, because, as Dad says, I was being spoiled by a slew of loving grandmothers.

After a while, I got to know some of the other kids at the day-care center. I considered them my friends, even though we'd usually only do group activities together. Otherwise, I tended to do my own thing.

At the center was a small electronic keyboard that I enjoyed playing on. One day as I played, one of my friends came by and sat next to me on the floor. "Patrick Henry," she said, "did you know you was blind?"

I had never really thought about it, so I said, "No, I didn't know." Then my friend asked me if I knew why I was blind.

I thought about that for a minute. "No."

"'Cause you were born that way."

"Oh," I said, and returned to my playing.

Did I know I was blind? At that time, I probably didn't know what the word *blind* meant. Did I know I couldn't see? That's not easy to answer, because I didn't know what it was to not see, having never seen anything. But I knew I was born without eyes and that I was going to have artificial eyes so that I'd look more like my parents.

When kids or adults would ask me about my blindness, I'd tend to shrug it off. I didn't feel emotional about it; it just *was*. Mom says the counselors at school were concerned that my blasé attitude about my blindness might mean I was in denial. The counselors wanted to work with me about my true feelings, help me get them out, and they wanted to do it without my parents being there. But Mom and Dad were worried that instead of helping, too much focus on my disabilities might convince me that something was wrong with me and that I would start feeling sorry for myself and making excuses. So, they didn't allow the counseling.

Mom knew how much I might be influenced by other peoples' attitudes, especially well-meaning adults. One time, I had been visiting some friends who didn't know how much I could do, and they wouldn't let me do anything for myself. That was fine with me, and when I came home, I wanted that pampering to continue. So, the next morning, when it came to things I normally did on my own and without a problem, like getting from the bed to my wheelchair, I started whining that I couldn't do it because I was crippled. Mom put her foot down and stopped that right quick. "Patrick Henry, I know you can do this," she said. "So cut the whining and get moving." I'm glad she did.

When people ask me what exactly do I "see" in my mind's eye, it's difficult to explain it and have it make sense. Think about trying to see with your elbow. If you tried, you'd see nothing, and that's what it's like for me.

People have asked me if blindness is like going through life with your eyes closed. "Is everything dark?" they'll ask. I don't know what dark is. Sounds strange, I know, but to understand dark, you'd have to experience light, and I don't have a clue. I understand all these terms as concepts explained to me—I know dark and light are opposites, that dark happens at night and sunlight during the day, and that they refer to qualities that I can't perceive, but that's it. I don't even know what shades and shadows look like, much less colors. So, I guess the best answer is, in my mind's eye, I see nothing. But I do experience.

How do I process information or know how things differ or are the same? Dad has helped me a lot with this by getting models for me. I can't get my arms around a car. I can feel parts of it, the hood, fender, bumper, or roof, but I'd have no idea of how a car was shaped if I couldn't hold a six-inch model in my hands. The same is true for a cow, an elephant, or a horse. Once I familiarize myself with a miniature version of something, I can imagine it being hundreds of times larger.

Touching the real thing is helpful. If I had a plastic model of a rhinoceros, I'd have a good idea of how it was shaped. But until I could feel its rough, leathery hide or the hide of another animal that was similar, my information about it would be woefully incomplete.

How do I create memories? I feel them, in a way that's probably pretty similar to what sighted people do, except I don't have any visual image of what happened. Visual memories are a high priority for sighted people; I know my parents remember best when they've seen something clearly, having created in their memory a fixed snapshot that they can call up and look at. But the other senses are used all the time, whether you are sighted or not. If you smelled a hot dog, but couldn't see it, and someone asked you what it was, from memory you'd know. You'd get a feeling of some sort and interpret it as "hot dog." Maybe you'd also associate that hot dog with a time, a place, an experience—eating it at the baseball game last summer. I do the same. Since I don't have visual memories, I think the memories I have based on my other senses may be more sensitive and detailed than those of a sighted person, although I have no way of knowing for sure.

When I got to public school and into the Head Start program, my being different was actually a pretty cool thing. All my classmates wanted to be my assistant, to help push me around in my wheelchair, and to make sure I had everything I needed. It got to the point where the teacher had to make up a chart that scheduled who was going to assist me each day. When the teacher would gather us in a circle to read to us, everyone wanted to sit beside me, and there'd be a mad rush to get to the right spots. So the teacher had to make up another chart that scheduled who was going to sit beside me, and when. At first, I loved all the attention. But later, as I came to realize why I was getting so much, it kind of backfired and I didn't want to be seen as so different.

Even though I still liked to spend my time with adults and my brothers, as I got to school age, it became increasingly more important to me that I be accepted by other kids my own age. My parents mainstreamed me in school. I had various assistants throughout school to make this possible, and I participated in every activity I could, from marching band to the prom. But no matter what you do, and however much others welcome you among them, the truth is, if you are "special," you can never be exactly like everyone else. And eventually I realized this is okay. When I started being noticed for my music and stage appearances, this allowed me to be recognized for being a different kind of special, the kind I wanted to be. Once I got it, I could let those other feelings go.

DAD

My son knew he couldn't see. But I'm not sure he knew exactly what that meant, especially as it might relate to others who *could* see, because he had never seen anything and had no point of reference. It was the same case with his standing and walking. I don't believe there was an epiphany, a specific point at which he realized he was different because he was blind. My wife and I, right or wrong, treated Patrick Henry the same way we'd treat any other child, including our other two sons. We, of course, explained why we were doing things, why we took him to an ocularist to be fitted with conformers, to therapists for special exercises and to have arm and leg braces made, to surgeons for multiple operations, and so forth. I'm sure we handled this in the same way parents of "normal" children explain the need for braces on teeth, or eyeglasses. These things simply needed to be done, as we parents like to say, "for your own good."

We thought the time would come when we'd have a big conversation about his issues, similar to having the big "birds and bees" talk with your children. But with Patrick Henry, nothing had yet triggered us to take that direction. Maybe that's why he wasn't very conscious of his condition at an early age and didn't dwell on his limitations.

Patrick Henry's blindness came to the forefront when other children his age were learning to read and print their letters and numbers, and it was time for our son to do the same. But he couldn't do it the way they did. He had to use coded dots he could feel with his fingertips. The only actual printing or writing he's ever done with a pen is his signature. I have to position the pen exactly on the line for him and tell him how much space he has. Some things you sign you have to squeeze your signature into a tiny space, like on a government form, while other things you sign are wide open.

PATRICK HENRY

My parents explained to me that I wouldn't be learning to read and print in the same way other kids in my classes did. "That's fine," I said. "I'd rather play my piano." Unfortunately, that's not what they were telling me. I still had to learn, but the way I would do it was called Braille.

I hated having to learn Braille, and I couldn't see the relevance. It was just a bunch of raised dots that didn't mean anything, and it took time that I could be using to play music. So to make it seem more like fun and a family kind of thing, my parents decided they'd learn right along with me at home.

There are different ways you can learn Braille. In the Grade 1 system, you learn all twenty-six letters of the alphabet in Braille, and use them the same way sighted people use Roman letters. The letters are shown as raised dots in groups, or cells, of from one to six dots. In the Grade 1 system, if you wanted to write the word *and*, you would use the three letters, *a, n,* and *d,* in Braille: ⠁ ⠝ ⠙. My parents and I started out with this method, and at first, Dad was gung ho about the whole thing. Grade 1 Braille is the slower method, but it's easier to learn, because all you have to do is learn twenty-six letters.

After a while, we moved on to learn Grade 2 Braille, which is used most often. You still have to learn the letters, but instead of using three different letters for a word like *and,* you'd use only one Braille character, called a contraction—a special design of dots. The word *and* is written ⠯. The same is true for words like *can, the, go, do, that,* and other words that are used a lot.

Grade 2 Braille is faster, once you get the hang of it, but in addition to learning twenty-six letters, you also have to learn about 250 contractions. It's complicated, and the materials we were using to learn at home didn't make things easier for my parents, who were struggling to understand it, much less use it. Dad didn't like Grade 2, and I'd hear him complaining about it to Mom. I started moving ahead of them because at school I had a Braille teacher, Miss Nettie Wolfe. But it took a while before I started making good progress.

I was still being stubborn, so early on, I thought I had worked out a scheme that would get me off the hook with Miss Nettie. She had me read one of my favorite books in Braille, Dr. Seuss's *The Cat in the Hat.* Granddaddy had read this to me so many times I had it perfectly memorized. So when she handed me the book and opened it to the first page, I pretended like I was reading. I ran my fingers over the dots and recited the words from memory, then I flipped to the next page. I didn't make one mistake, but she caught on to what I was doing after just a couple of pages. In thinking back on this, I was probably going much faster than I should have if I was really reading the dots.

"Patrick Henry," Miss Nettie said firmly, "you are supposed to be reading the words on the page, not telling me what's going on in the story from your memory. That won't help you."

I couldn't see how learning Braille would help me, either, but I was busted. I knew I'd have to buckle down and start learning this stuff. But I didn't give up my subversive ways. I had always been successful with adults at changing the subject, and I assumed this would work with Miss Nettie. So when she had my daily lesson all mapped out in front of us and ready to go, I started asking questions that I hoped would take us down a long, different path.

"Miss Nettie, who invented Braille?"

"The system was first started by a soldier, a captain in the French army in the early 1800s named Charles Barbier. He called it *night writing*. It was supposed to allow soldiers to pass information back and forth without talking and without a light at night."

"So, why isn't it called Barbier?"

"Mr. Barbier's system was too complicated, and the army rejected it. It would have died right then if Louis Braille had not discovered it and perfected it."

I was ready with my next question when she said, "Now, Patrick Henry, I think it's time we moved on to our lesson of the day. If you like, we can continue the history lesson on Louis Braille when we've finished our work."

Mom said I'd come home every day complaining about "that mean old Miss Nettie." This made my parents curious and a little nervous about what was going on, so they came to the school to meet her. Dad laughed when they were introduced, because to him she was the sweetest lady. Better yet, she was one step ahead of me and I couldn't pull any of my diversionary tactics on her. Busted again.

Things got better in a hurry once I put my mind to learning Braille. That, plus Miss Nettie did something really neat that turned me on to the process. We started using flash cards that worked like scratch-and-sniff stationery. She would give me a card, and I'd run my fingers over the dots and tell her what I had read. Maybe it was the word *red,* the color, which, of course meant nothing to me. But then I could scratch the card and there would be the fragrance of cherry. It gave me an association of the word *red* with something real, something that in a world I couldn't see actually *was* red. We did the same for the word *yellow,* which smelled like a pineapple, and *green,* which smelled like mint. I loved this and couldn't get enough of it.

DAD

When it comes to Patrick Henry, there's nothing Patricia and I wouldn't do to make his life better. That included our attempting Braille. People we talked to thought this was important, in the same way that family members should learn sign language if they have a deaf child. We were told we couldn't rely solely on the school program to teach him as well as he'd need to learn, and working at home on his Braille was thought to be equally important. There also was the practical issue of being able to leave notes for one another and things like that. The more we learned about it, the more it seemed that we'd be negligent parents if we didn't learn Braille.

We started with some material from the Hadley School for the Blind in Chicago, learning the ABCs, the basics of Grade 1 Braille. It was hard for all of us, but harder for me and Patricia because we have vision. We were told that the same part of the brain is used for reading by sight and by touch, so when you're used to seeing words and start trying to read by touch alone, you can get confused. Patrick Henry didn't have that problem, and he learned much faster than we did. That struck us as ironic, because we were supposed to be the ones helping him along.

As Patricia and I struggled, we'd remind each other that nothing worth doing comes without hard work and perseverance. So, we hung in there, while getting further and further behind our son, especially since he was learning so much more working with Nettie Wolfe in the Head Start program. She was a wonderful teacher, perfect for Patrick Henry, and as he moved along, his learning seemed to accelerate, leaving us in the dust. At that point, I saw no purpose for torturing myself any longer, and I threw in the towel. Patricia hung on longer, but that was typical for us back then.

PATRICK HENRY

My other senses are probably more important to me than they are to people who can see. Because I could play the piano at such a young age and I have a highly sensitive ear for musical notes and tones, you'd think my hearing would be the sense that tells me the most about the world. It is crucial, that's for sure, but my hearing is so sensitive it can be a problem.

As much as I love music, I used to hate the "Happy Birthday" song. The sudden loudness afterward—all the whooping and applause—would freak me out when I was young. I hated opening presents at birthday parties, too, knowing everyone would be making an uproar each time I got the wrapping paper off. I remember the birthday of one of my day-care teachers. She tried everything to get me to sing "Happy Birthday" to her, even going so far as to start singing the song herself, over and over again, hoping I would join in. I wouldn't sing it for anything. I realize now I probably hurt her feelings, and I wish I had just sung it and then held my ears.

Even after I came to expect the explosion of noise after this song, I still hated it. Then I noticed that folks would applaud and make an uproar after I played the piano or sang. Mom explained that this meant they appreciated my talents and they were telling me so with their applause and whistling. Suddenly, that was a different matter entirely, and I started to like it and wanted more.

My hearing is important to me, but I think touch may be

even more so as a source of information. I can hear a bird sing, but touching it and feeling it in my hands tells me a lot more about birds. I love to go to a petting zoo and feel the animals. So many different types of hair, fur, hide, and skin, each with its own unique qualities, identity, and purpose.

When I was a little kid, I had a collection of stuffed animals I took to bed every night. Mom laughs about how systematic I have always been about things, even back then. She would hand me each animal, one at a time, I'd feel it and know instantly which one it was, hug it and place it beside me just right, and wait for the next one. Each one had a name, and I would play and whisper to them when my parents put me to bed. I'd keep going for hours, maybe until three A.M. Then, when I woke up the next morning, I'd be tired. Mom and Dad got worried that something might be wrong with me, because they knew I was going to bed early and should be getting plenty of sleep. Then one night, they waited just outside my room to see if they could figure out what was going on. Sure enough, they heard me talking to my stuffed toys. After that, I had a rule at night to tell all my animals, "No games."

Touch is really important to me, but sometimes when you can't see what you are touching, it can get you into trouble. One time, Mom and I were sitting on the front porch steps. I liked to wait for an ambulance to pass by so I could hear the siren. Right below where I was sitting was the yard; I dangled my arm and felt what I thought was a piece of hair on the grass. I wondered how the hair got there. But it wasn't hair. It was a bumblebee lying quiet and still, on my index finger. Then I tried to put my thumb on top of it to hold on to it. The bee didn't like that. I know, because I felt a terrible pain, a pain I had never felt before. I yelped—my first bee sting. Mom doctored me up.

My sense of smell helps me, too, especially when it comes to food. But when Mom would make dinner, although I could smell what she was cooking, I really wanted to feel it. I wanted to feel the steam from something boiling on the stove, the texture of a piece of raw chicken or steak, the ice on the frozen vegetables before they were cooked, the heat from the oven when cookies were being baked.

When I was younger, I would always ask folks if I could feel their face with my hands. One time, I asked this of a lady who came up to meet us after one of our performances. She said, "Okay, but you're going to get lipstick all over your fingers." She didn't know that I only wanted to touch her along her jaw line and maybe around her eyes a little bit. I love shaking hands and feeling the skin on the arm, whether it's the smooth skin of a younger person or the more wrinkled skin of someone older, whether it's tough like someone working out of doors, or soft like an accountant. And, of course, hugs and a kiss on the cheek are the best feelings of all.

In this book, there is a lot written about Dad and all the wonderful things he does and how much he has sacrificed for me. Dad and I are the most visible members of our family, in the marching band on the football field and in performances all over the country. But my mom is the one who deserves the most credit. She took up my cause from day one. When I was born, there was no manual on how to care for me. She didn't know where to start, so she called everyone she could think of and ended up at VIPS, Visually Impaired Preschool Services. She says they were a Godsend and helped give her confidence that she could do what was necessary. She's the one who tracked down the specialists who worked on me, and she made sure they were the right ones. She wanted someone who was adept at doing surgery, but who would also talk to her and tell her what she needed to know. It was constant trial and error, but Mom made sure I was getting all the resources I needed to develop to the best of my ability. I can't thank her enough.

The most impressive thing about Mom is not just how much she accomplishes in any given day, but that you'd never know she was the one who did it. I hate to admit it, but my brothers and I take so much of what she does for granted. If there was a big pile of bricks out in front of the house that needed to be moved, Mom would do it at midnight and no one would ever know she did it or how hard she worked. If my brothers and I had to do the same task, we'd work hard to get it done, but we'd also expect Mom to show up every fifteen minutes, bringing us cookies and cold lemonade, and telling us again and again what a wonderful job we were doing.

DAD

Patricia is the one who should be telling this part of the story about all the things she went through early in Patrick Henry's life. But if she did, this passage would be amazingly short, because she wouldn't want it to appear as if she were bragging. She'd leave out all the details and make it seem like she did only a little. Far from it.

Patricia researched an infinite number of questions, which is more difficult than you might think if you don't even know what questions to ask, and she did it all from scratch. In those days, there was no Google that would search through millions of Web sites for you, or guidebooks on how to proceed. When Patrick Henry was first born, Patricia would be on the phone all day long, tracking down anyone who might be of help on the issue of the moment. Then when she went back to work, she still applied the same amount of energy to our son's cause. She'd make calls from work on her lunch hour and breaks; then she'd come home and get back on the phone. Continually she would hear, "Please hold," "Sorry, but I'm going to have to transfer you," "I don't know why they referred you to this office," "No, I don't know who might be able to help you." Another dead end. But she never faltered or backed down.

She paved the way to doctor's offices, surgeons, physical therapists, and all sorts of counselors, checking on referrals and not taking anything for granted. She did the homework on how to go about getting resources, learning aids, and appropriate strategies we should apply; she looked into the

Head Start program and lining up an acceptable day-care center. Patricia insisted we follow up the lead on the ocularist in Indianapolis, even though it might be a wild-goose chase, not to mention driving the 120 miles one way from Louisville. She led the charge on our learning Braille and kept me motivated when I'd get so frustrated I wanted to scream.

From the beginning, one of her primary concerns was how to train and teach our son to maximize his ability to function in our society. She had no idea, of course, what his potential was, and there was no one who could tell her, because Patrick Henry was so unique. But she decided that "if Helen Keller could learn, then he can, too." Thank God for Visually Impaired Preschool Services, which turned out to be a fantastic resource. The organization gave us information about so many things, but one of the most helpful was how to teach Patrick Henry at home to heighten his sensitivity to his environment and sharpen his other senses to be more valuable to him. Staff members taught us how we sighted people don't even register how much information we can absorb with just one quick glance. And because we take it for granted, it never occurs to us how much a blind person is missing. It's incredible.

Take something simple like watching his mom prepare dinner. For Patrick Henry, each step needs to be explained in detail. "We are entering the kitchen. I'm opening the refrigerator door. A light comes on in the refrigerator so that I can see what's in it. I'm reaching in for the milk. I'm taking the carton to the table and pouring the liquid into a glass. I'm turning on the gas on the burner of the stove—careful, keeping my hand away because the flame could burn me—and placing a skillet on it, and now I'm putting the cuts of meat into the skillet. Ok, now the meat is beginning to sizzle . . ." And so on.

Just walking through the house required explanation. "I am walking into the living room. I am switching on the ceiling light. I'm walking on a hardwood floor, and now I'm on carpet." It took us awhile to be able to think through each activity without leaving out key elements that would be important to Patrick Henry. Sometimes he'd ask a question, and we'd realize that we had failed to provide a bridge between A and B. Because we were so visually familiar with it, we had overlooked it.

Patricia was carrying a heavy load back then, and it was made even heavier by the thoughtless words or actions of others. People don't mean to insult, but it still stung when someone would refer to Patrick Henry as "that deformed baby." Or when they'd give him a pitiful look and ask a question like, "Can he even smile?" When asked this question, she responded as politely as she could, but I'm sure with a considerable strain in her voice. "Of course he can smile! He's blind, not paralyzed! And he's a very happy baby, and he smiles when he wants to, just like all babies."

And there are the people who mean well, those who have never had to deal with what we were facing. Still, they wanted to give Patricia all kinds of advice on situations they knew nothing about. She had to cope with some experts who talked down to her, who seemed to think that we had no common sense or ability to solve problems. Her role as a parent was to accept everything she was told as if it were gospel. Not all the experts were like that, of course, and some were compassionate and great.

I was unaware of how much of this type of treatment Patricia had experienced and how much it had built up inside her until she opened up about it one night. As she allowed a few tears to flow, I tried to comfort her. Then something unusual happened, unusual for her. She exploded. Something inside her had reached the boiling point, and it just had to come out. "You know what?" she cried. "I'm strong! I'm facing challenges people can't even imagine, and I'm coping. I am handling it. Maybe my son is not progressing like other children, and maybe he won't be a star athlete or a great brain surgeon someday. Maybe he'll never even reach the lofty perch of being average, like all the rest. But I'll tell you this . . . he'll be *everything* he's able to be."

I remember how, after her outburst, I just stared at her. She had surprised me, and I loved it. I knew she was coping about as well as anyone could, but to see her this strong told me that nothing was going to keep any of us down for long.

Where did my wife get her incredible strength? Patricia's grandmother, "Mammaw," still alive and feisty at eighty-four, was her primary role model. Mammaw raised seven children—four girls and three boys—and did it mostly on her own. She owned a restaurant in the downtown Louisville area not far from where Patricia grew up. At the time, this area wasn't a great neighborhood. Mammaw fed most of the city's winos for years. Sometimes, they'd pay her, but mostly she fed them for free. She'd say, "Where else are they going to eat?" Mammaw had a big heart, but she was no pushover. These characteristics are what I see in my wife.

Patricia believes there's no time or place for self-pity. When life knocks you on the ground, you pick yourself up and move on, because no one else will do it for you. She's passed along this attitude to Patrick Henry, and it shows in just about everything he does.

Something that also helped us at that time was the realization that other parents of more typical children have their own particular problems and worries. They fret about how well their children are doing in school and what college they'll attend, or how well they're doing on the playing field. For us, it was becoming more apparent day by day that we were blessed by just concentrating on the most basic human elements—simply loving our son without getting caught up in the trivial matters that preoccupy so many parents. What's more, we were able to see each small victory with Patrick Henry as another one of God's miracles.

PATRICK HENRY

I got a taste of what Mom had to go through in dealing with how unkind some folks can be. People would make assumptions about me. I'd hear them say things in front of me as if I wasn't there or wasn't smart enough to understand I was being talked about. This still happens. No big deal. I remember one time after I had spoken to an audience and then sung a song that brought down the house, someone came up and stood right in front of me, then asked Dad, "How old is he?" As they got used to this treatment, my parents started handling it better. They'd simply deflect such questions by saying, "Let's ask *him.*"

I didn't know it, of course, but people sometimes would stare at me, even though Mom or Dad was standing right beside me. Not all these encounters were offensive. Kids sometimes have unusual reactions to me, and some are humorous. One day, we were at a ball game, and this little kid came up very close to me; at one point, we were almost nose to nose. Then he backed up a little, but he kept staring. Dad had had enough of this and was about to say something, when the kid blurted out, "What's wrong with his hair?" Dad and I laughed.

Sometimes, we'd experience folks' simple ignorance of how to handle my disabilities. I know that there will always be rules in the world and they need to be followed, but I think that sometimes, they can be taken a little too far. As you know, I love the scary rides in amusement parks, but to ride them, you have to be at least a certain height. After my back operation, I knew I was tall enough for the rides that required me to be at least forty-eight inches, and besides, I would be going on the rides with my father. But when Dad and I got in line at one park to ride the roller coaster, they wouldn't let us on. So he took me straight to the main office and tried to explain the situation, but they didn't know what to do with me. Dad was determined.

"If you don't believe he's tall enough, let's measure him," he said.

Measuring my height isn't easy, so Dad had me lie on the floor, and he stretched me out as far as he could. They got a tape measure, and from the tip of my head to my toes, I was exactly forty-eight inches. Only then did they give me a wristband that would allow me to get on the rides.

To be fair, we've encountered countless people who have been gracious and have treated me just like anyone else. Thankfully, these folks are by far in the majority. Dr. Greg Byrne, the director of the University of Louisville marching band; the marching band members; the crew who worked on our new home for the *Extreme Makeover: Home Edition* television program; folks who invite us to talk and perform; people we meet in stores when we're out shopping; musicians, teachers, medical professionals—the list goes on. These people get it; they understand that I'm more like them than I am different from them. I thrive on acceptance and being thought of as a valuable human being and not someone to be pitied. So, the next time you meet someone who strikes you as being different, go in the opposite direction and look for all the ways the person is just like you.

DAD

From the earliest months of Patrick Henry's life, I didn't fully grasp the many challenges we'd have to face as parents. Patricia, on the other hand, knew the depth of our situation right from the start. She also knew that for the most part, she'd be doing this alone or, at best, dragging me along behind her.

Once we adjusted to life with Patrick Henry, I quickly moved back into my old lifestyle. My attitude was, *Everything's fine, and I'm sure it will be whether I'm there or not.* I played softball two days a week, bowled one night, played basketball another night, and went to my lodge every other Friday. These were my scheduled events. I also had to have free time to do whatever I wanted on the spur of the moment. If you do a quick calculation, it's easy to see that between my work and play, I wasn't home very often. But how was it possible that I could be so carefree, with all that was required at home to care for a baby like Patrick Henry? The answer is Patricia. Mom did it all. And more than that, she gave me credit for being a good father, someone who really did care, in spite of my immature ways.

Thankfully, I felt like a responsible father at least sometimes. One of the nicest things I enjoyed when Patrick Henry was an infant was naps with him on the sofa. He has always been a hugger. I would lie on my back on the sofa, watching TV, and I would lay Patrick Henry on my chest, face down with my hands on his back. This was the best bonding for me I could imagine. At these times, Patrick Henry was not blind or disabled. He was just my son on my chest.

From about the age of two years on, after we picked him up from day care, Patricia would start dinner and Patrick Henry would play with his basket of toys. He'd take them out one at a time, play with each one for a few minutes, then set it aside. When the basket was empty, he'd put it on his head and roll around the room exploring. We'd eat dinner, then he'd take a bath, play a little more, read books, and listen to a bedtime tape before bed. He was really a wonderful child. Of course, when I'd comment on this, Patricia would just nod and give me one of her looks. The kind that says, "Like you'd know."

We knew of fathers whose baby had been born with problems and who, as a result, left their wives. The men couldn't handle having a child who was less than perfect, and they didn't want anything to do with raising it. By comparison, since not being there never occurred to me, you could say I looked pretty good. That, of course, is about the lowest standard anyone could apply, and in looking back, I'm not proud that not running away was the best I could do.

Patricia gave me a free pass most of the time, with one exception: the Corvette.

It was 1998, and we had three young boys, including one in diapers, and Patrick Henry, who at ten, still needed considerable help with everyday tasks, especially after his back surgery. Somehow, I decided this would be a good time to fulfill a lifelong dream and buy a 1984 Corvette, the only kind I could afford. Actually, we couldn't afford it at all—it took a second mortgage and maxing out credit cards to stretch and make ends meet—but a golfing buddy of mine helped me avoid feeling guilt about the purchase. He'd tell me you only live once, so you'd better grab all you can.

My "Vette" was the first model in the C-4 series. Don't

ever buy the first model in a series, because there are too many bugs to be worked out, and my Vette had constant problems. As if the purchase price and the astonishingly high insurance rates that go along with driving one of these beauties weren't enough, there were repair bills you wouldn't believe. A friend had to bring me home once, because I had been out hot-rodding and blew the transmission. Patricia didn't say a word, but her look told me she was silently livid.

I was away from home six out of seven nights. It pains me to write this now, but when she'd mention needing help or that she'd appreciate my being home a little more often, I'd throw it back in her face. "You're the one who wanted children, and now you got 'em. Deal with it!" Then I'd take off in my Corvette.

Despite Patricia's heroic efforts, my marriage was deteriorating and close to being ruined. I know now that many women tend to try to make things work, while many men head toward the exit when things start getting rough. Then, when the smoke clears, men want to come back. But if the woman hangs on until she's completely exhausted and has to quit, there's no turning back. She's gone for good. Thankfully, Patricia didn't reach that point.

Ironically, even though Patrick Henry required so much from Patricia, I think it was because of him that she gave our marriage more rope and, fortunately for me, was able to hang on longer. Patrick Henry had become a stabilizing force in our household. He gave her strength when she felt beaten down, and through him, she saw in me something that I didn't know was there. Ultimately, she had faith that it would rise to the surface if she gave it enough time and invested enough love.

Finally, even with my blinders on and my best efforts to avoid confronting reality, I slowly realized that we needed a minivan for the family. The only way we could afford one was if I let the Corvette go. Patricia never said a word, but everything about her said, this was it: the Corvette or the family.

I remember I had started going back to church around that time, and I even had started praying more for guidance. Well, be careful of what you pray for, because everything in my life pointed toward an end to the Corvette era. I sold it; we bought a minivan. At the time, that was a real blow to my macho persona. But deep down, I was glad that for once, I had done the right thing.

I love all my boys. Jesse was a good athlete, and I enjoyed going to his games and watching him excel. Cameron was a delightful baby. But I found myself feeling an increasing kinship with Patrick Henry. Even though he was completely dependent on us to meet his physical needs, he imparted to me a sense that there was more to life than my keyhole view of the world.

Combining the loving forces of my family, I began to grow. With each step I took, my past life played in my mind like a newsreel, one bad dream after another, in the way they say your whole life passes in front of you when you die. When it came to reviewing what a jerk I had been, I had a lot of material to cover. But what a blessing it was that I could soon talk to Patricia about many of these transgressions. She'd laugh about them, instead of holding a grudge. And Patrick Henry, of course, always accepted me as I was and loved me without question.

PATRICK HENRY

When I think about my family, I think about a structure with four major parts, and each part is distinct in its own way. There is Dad (the provider); me, Patrick Henry (the musician); Jesse (the superathlete); and Cameron (the stand-up comic). But there's a fifth element that is not so obvious and is not appreciated unless it's missing. It's the glue that holds the parts together. Mom is the glue.

I love my Mom; she's incredible in so many ways. But I know that even though I can be a ham onstage, I'm not usually the demonstrative type. And if I'm honest, I'm not sure I even know everything she's done on my behalf, but I know it's a lot. Maybe when we're older, my brothers and I will finally be able to adequately express just how much we appreciate her. Until then, I'm sure Mom is the one who's the least concerned about that. Knowing we all are doing well and doing it together is what's most important to her.

Be the You *Your Mother Would Be Proud Of*

PATRICK HENRY

My mother has high standards, which she doesn't compromise, and she never asks more of others than she is ready and willing to do herself. This applies to me, too, even though folks might think she'd greatly reduce her expectations of me. Ha-ha! Mom never cut me too much slack. From the beginning, when it came to me, Mom's motto was, "He'll be everything he's able to be." And she sure saw to that.

My mother's expectations of me are the same ones she applies to my brothers, and I think those expectations are probably similar to those that every loving mother places on her children. Mom believes if you go through life with a positive attitude and a good-faith effort, what you accomplish will take care of itself and be enough. How long it might take me to learn Braille, or how good I might be at it, wasn't as important as my trying as hard as I could. The same is true for my schoolwork, my music, my therapy exercises, and my efforts toward mastering everyday tasks that will help me be more independent. I've never felt any pressure to do more than I can, but I'm always expected to do all that I can.

At the end of the day, can you look back and say to yourself, "Today, my mother would be proud of me because I gave it all I had?" If you can, you will have had a very good day. And if you can do this every day, you will have a very good life. I'm proof of that.

Chapter 5

The Best Personal Heroes Can Be Found Close to Home

*So in everything, do to others
what you would have them do to you.*

—MATTHEW 7:12

PATRICK HENRY

Sometimes in e-mails or in person, people will share their lives with me, telling me how I've inspired them to keep going when times were tough. Some have told me I'm their hero. I don't often know how to respond, because that isn't how I view myself, though I'm honored that someone would see me in that way. But honestly, when I think of a hero, one person comes to mind: my father.

Dad isn't incredible in the ways you would ordinarily imagine heroes to be. He's never caught a criminal, run into a burning building, or saved anyone's life. He doesn't make championship-winning shots at the buzzer. And he hasn't done anything famous that I know of. He works nights at

UPS, doesn't make a lot of money, and is pretty much just an everyday kind of guy, tall and thin and bald.

But what he does every day is so much bigger and more difficult. He'll never be a weight lifter or pro-football lineman, but Dad has true strength, because he's had the courage to put his own life on hold and sacrifice everything so that another human being, me, can live a better life. These days, he gives all his time, energy, and support to his family, asking nothing in return. No doubt many other individuals in the world today are doing the kinds of things my father does, quietly giving all they have to others. I'm just thankful Dad happens to be one of them.

I know I'm biased because I'm his son, but I rarely see him taking any credit. If what he does comes up in conversation, he steers it somewhere else. If pushed, he'll admit he helps me complete some tasks and does some for me, but is quick to point out that any parent would do the same. I know a lot of wonderful people, but I often wonder if they could handle what my parents do for even one week.

Dad isn't a particularly religious man in the traditional sense, not the kind who goes around spouting Bible verses. But he has always instilled in me a deep faith in God. Throughout my life, when things were tough for me—like recuperating from my surgeries—I'd take comfort in Dad's faith and strength, knowing he was there with an encouraging word, feeling everything I felt, fighting each battle right beside me.

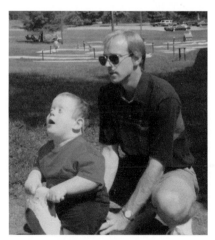

TOP: In my crib with my "friends." I'm fifteen months old. ABOVE LEFT: At my mom's family reunion, Rough River State Park, Kentucky. RIGHT: On the phone with Granny and Granddaddy; four years old.

ABOVE: Making music with my brother Jesse in our living room, fall 1994. Jesse is three, and I'm six. LEFT: With my new brother Cameron, August 1995. Cam is one month old; I'm seven. BELOW: At an amusement park, summer of 1994. Jesse is three, and I'm six. I loved amusement park rides even then.

LEFT: Metro United Way Campaign photo of me at my keyboard, September 1995. I'm seven years old. (*Photo by Metro United Way*)

ABOVE: United Way photo with Dad and Granddaddy, fall 1995. I'm seven years old. (*Photo by Metro United Way*) LEFT: On the backyard sky fort with my brothers, spring of 1996. Cam is almost one year old, Jesse is five, and I'm eight.

TOP: Family Christmas photo, December 1998.
BOTTOM: Having fun with Granddaddy!

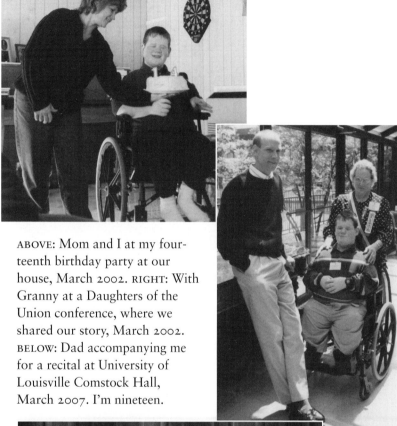

ABOVE: Mom and I at my fourteenth birthday party at our house, March 2002. RIGHT: With Granny at a Daughters of the Union conference, where we shared our story, March 2002. BELOW: Dad accompanying me for a recital at University of Louisville Comstock Hall, March 2007. I'm nineteen.

University of Louisville versus Pittsburgh at
Heinz Field in Pittsburgh, November 25, 2006.
(*Photo by Mark Hawkins*)

University of Louisville band at Churchill Downs on Kentucky
Derby Day, May 2007. Dr. Byrne is on the ladder.

ABOVE: Bus driver—move that bus! November 2007. RIGHT: Seeing my new *Extreme Makeover: Home Edition* home on the outside. BELOW: With my University of Louisville band mates at the reveal of the new marching band field, November 2007. (*Photos © American Broadcasting Companies, Inc.*)

TOP: With my family, Dr. Byrne, and Ty Pennington during the marching band field reveal, November 2007. (*Photo © American Broadcasting Companies, Inc.*) BOTTOM: In front of our brand new *Extreme Makeover: Home Edition* home, November 2007.

Dad really stepped up for me when I started college at the University of Louisville. Even though the Disability Resources Center at the university could help me, offering to hire an assistant to push me to my classes and do other things I needed help with, Dad was concerned it wouldn't be nearly enough. So he signed on to be my legs and eyes on campus. Dad was right. I'm now in my junior year, and without him, I don't know if I could have made it through. It certainly would have been a very different experience, and for sure not as much fun.

Here's what a typical day is like for us:

8:50 A.M.: Dad's day starts at precisely this time in the morning. That doesn't sound too bad, but wait until you see how it goes before you decide if you'd like to trade places with him. He tries to sleep until the very last minute if he can. Then he jumps out of bed to come for me at the piano, first thing. He's knows I've been there a while, because Mom has to leave early for work. Before she goes, she makes me breakfast and pushes me through the house to the piano, so that I can practice before school starts. Dad pushes me back to my room to get dressed. We gather up what books I'll need for my classes, and we get ready to leave the house.

9:45 A.M.: Dad grabs a cup of coffee, and we head out the door. The first challenge is getting me into the van. We don't have a hydraulic lift, so Dad has to push me up to the sliding door and lift me into the captain's chair. As I keep getting bigger, I'm a heavier load for Dad to lift. But he never says anything about it, like, "Son, you've got to cut back on those chocolate chip cookies," and he doesn't complain. I wiggle into a comfortable position and put on my seat belt. Then he takes my wheelchair to the other side of the van and puts it in a space where another captain's chair used to be. My wheelchair doesn't collapse and fold up, because it was specially designed for me. It has been reinforced to be stronger and take a beating, plus there's a sturdy rack underneath the seat for my books and trumpet.

During my first term at the university, I had classes every day, Monday through Friday, the first starting at 11:00 A.M. It's only about a twenty-minute drive to campus, but we tried to leave no later than 10:15, because traffic is unpredictable, as is how far away we might have to park. We have a handicapped sticker for the van, but there aren't many spaces, and some folks don't care and park there, anyway. If there's a spot on campus, great, our morning is easier. If not, we have to drive in circles along with thousands of other commuters hurrying to class. And if we find a nonhandicapped space, Dad has to lift me out of the van before he can pull in, because there won't be room on the sides to unload me and the chair. This usually stops traffic. Rainy days are the worst, since even with an umbrella, my wheelchair and I can get soaked fast.

11 A.M.–4:30 P.M.: Dad takes me to my first class and sits beside me. As I listen to a lecture, I can take notes on my Braille note-taker. It works like a laptop computer, except it has a Braille keyboard, and I can type pretty fast on it and keep up

with everyone else. It's a little distracting to the other students at first, because when I hit the keys firmly, it makes some noise. I like having Dad there beside me to explain what's going on in the room—if the professor puts up a graph, is showing a visual on-screen, or gives us a handout. Dad also tells me when something funny happens and what the others are laughing about.

My major is Spanish, and I don't have a minor. I take four classes per term, the minimum to be considered full time, and it's about all we can do with the many things going on in my life and Dad's. I love my Spanish classes where we discuss Spanish culture, arts, and literature; doing translations; and, of course, learning to be fluent in the language. I take two Spanish classes each term, and in just my second year, I was already taking senior-level and graduate classes. Other than Spanish, I like classes on theology—my favorite was "Survey of Christian Thought and Culture." The other liberal arts courses, like history and such, are fine, but are not my favorites. And although I hate to admit it, I don't like chemistry or physics at all. Nor do I care much for English. When I got through these classes my freshman year and knew I didn't have to take any more of them, I was relieved.

Math classes are in a separate category for me. I call them torture. I can get A's in math classes because I can memorize algebraic formulas and can solve problems if I concentrate enough, but I guess I just don't see the relevance to anything. Even the math class I had that was practical and taught students how to compute compound interest on savings accounts, mortgage rates, and payments—things like that—I still had a hard time appreciating. When I complained, Dad actually agreed with me. "That's what accountants are for," he said.

I know Dad enjoys following along when the professor is good and the topic is interesting. Dad even likes my Spanish classes and is trying to improve his skills there. But like me, there are some classes he doesn't care for. If the class is long and I'm sure I won't need him, sometimes he can duck out to the van or the student lounge for a quick nap.

After the first class, we grab a bite to eat. There are several restaurants on campus if we have enough time. Otherwise, Dad will grab some snacks from the vending machine or he might bring sandwiches from home. Then we're off to the rest of my classes.

4:30–6:30 P.M.: After a full day, it's time to head to the marching band practice field on the other side of campus. Dad needs to be awake for this, to pay close attention to push me through all the formations without banging into other band members. During practices, Dad does all the work. Nobody else in the band has to push a clumsy chair and a guy my size around (together, it's about two hundred pounds), keeping one eye on the band leader and the other on where everyone else is going. Sometimes, practice goes long if we are working on a new routine or if it's close to game day. By the end, I'm feeling fine—all I've done is sit and play the trumpet. But I know Dad's exhausted.

7:00–8:00 P.M.: By the time we drive home and get cleaned

up, we're starving. Thankfully, we can count on Mom having cooked something great for us to eat.

8:00–10:00 P.M.: Then it's time to deal with homework. Textbook publishers have special programs that allow me to put the text on my computer and hear it, much like an audio book. But it always takes three weeks into the term for us to get this stuff, because the bookstore has to contact the publisher with the correct book number and verify that the textbook has been purchased and there is a special need. Every semester, we've tried to streamline this process without any luck. So, for the first three weeks, our only option is for Dad to read everything to me. I know he's tired and this just adds to it, sitting there reading out loud from a textbook for a couple of hours. Fortunately, I can read my Braille notes, or if I'm really tired, I can have the machine read them back to me. I prefer reading it myself, because the machine sometimes mispronounces, and after a while, the robotic tone gets annoying.

When I have a written assignment, I'll know what to do by listening in class. There's also usually a handout with details that Dad will read to me. Then I'm on my own unless I need help finding resources. Dad will take me to the library, where we'll talk to the reference librarian. Or, if need be, Dad will help me find things in the textbook. But the thinking and the writing are entirely up to me. When I prepare the final product to be turned in, I have two options. I can type it on my computer, like everyone else, and then have my voice software read it back to me to make sure it's correct.

Or, my Braille note-taker can convert what I've written in Braille to a computer file that can then be printed.

The people Dad works for at UPS have been really great. A few times, he had so much to do for me so that I could complete my assignments, he had to call in and miss work. There just wasn't any other way, because even though Mom can help me sometimes, she is equally busy helping and shuttling my two brothers, working full-time herself, cooking, and doing everything else to run the household.

10:00–10:30 P.M.: After my homework is done, Dad may have a little free time, so he tries to catch some of the news on TV while answering as many e-mails and letters as he can. My parents are very serious about answering mail. They view as precious every personal note someone takes the time to send, and they are honored to get them, so they try to answer every one. Sometimes, like after television appearances on *Oprah,* or the *Extreme Makeover: Home Edition* program, we got so many e-mails that by the time Dad answered one, we had received four more. I know it took him months to get caught up, if he ever did.

10:30 P.M.–4:00 A.M.: Dad has to be at work at 11:00 at night, so he grabs another cup of coffee and is out the door just as the rest of us are going to bed. His job is "auditor in revenue and recovery." He says it's a fancy name for what he does—standing at the conveyor belt as the larger packages come by and examining them. If something isn't packaged the way it's supposed to be, he pulls it off and scans it. This tells UPS the package is irregularly shaped, not square or rectangular as they require. He likes it when he's busy, and he usually is, because it helps keep him awake.

Before he got that job, he drove a tug, pulling a four-tiered wagon—the kind you see moving luggage to planes at the airport. He liked driving a tug, but it was thirty hours a week and he had to cut back to twenty hours when I started school, so he shifted inside to his scanning job.

His work at UPS is nothing glamorous and not what he saw himself doing when he was younger. But Dad likes to put things into perspective. "If it wasn't for my shift, I wouldn't be able to do everything I do with you, Patrick," he says. I know he means it, but I'm sure that when he gets home at 4:00 in the morning, knowing he's only going to get four and a half hours of sleep at best before the alarm goes off, his thoughts aren't about how perfect his job is.

On the weekends, Dad gets to sleep in a little. That is, unless we've been invited to perform out of town, which nowadays is pretty likely. If so, he's up earlier than usual, packing the van, and off we go, sometimes driving many hours to get to the event. It might be a small church in a rural area; other times, it's a corporate function in a major city. Whether there are twenty folks there or two thousand, we feel blessed to be asked.

Maybe I shouldn't admit it, but some days, I'd rather do anything but study. It's late, I'm tired, and I would rather just listen to music or a TV game show. And some days, after classes, I really don't want to go to marching band practice. If I feel this way, I can imagine how Dad must feel, having done the same as me, plus haul me around all day, not to mention his job at night, and on so little sleep. But he never complains to me. Thinking about what's going on with Dad gives me a quick reality check, and it gets me in the right mind-set to keep pushing forward.

On top of all he does for me, he makes sure my brothers get their fair share of him, too. He takes them golfing when he can, he attends their football or baseball games, and if either Cameron or Jesse have a school event that involves parents, Dad is there. One month, Dad and I were traveling so much, he felt bad he always had to leave Cameron behind (Jesse is old enough to drive now and takes care of himself, pretty much). So one weekend, Dad packed up the van and took Cameron to Florida, just the two of them, for a little getaway.

It's a miracle my father can do everything he does, and it gives me the message once again that if he can make the time, so can I.

Dad

I'm thrilled my son thinks of me as a hero. How many fathers can say they have that kind of relationship? But, really, I'm no more of a hero than any other parent who loves his son and wants the best for him. Sure, I've had to make some adjustments in my lifestyle to accommodate my son's special needs, but I believe anyone in my shoes would do the same if it was necessary. The truth is, I'm just an average guy who's been blessed to have a son who is anything but average.

Patrick Henry is the real hero in our family. There are so many reasons why, it's hard to know where to begin. Maybe the best place is at home.

Patrick Henry likes to say that things are "no big deal!" But if you were to follow him around for a day and witness the nitty-gritty aspects of his life, you'd see that his challenges are relentless and will always be there, confronting him. What he goes through every day *is* a big deal. And although I see this every day and live with it, I still marvel not only at what he does, but also at his amazing attitude about it.

I've never seen Patrick Henry down on life or feeling sorry for himself. He's patient as Job. Frequently, he has to wait for someone either to move him or to do something he can't do for himself, and there's a long list of such tasks. He'll just calmly sit, knowing that eventually it'll happen. Many times, I wouldn't realize he needed help and he'd been waiting a long time, but he wouldn't be annoyed. He'd be smiling and grateful, anyway. I wish I had even a fraction of his patience.

Until we got our new home this year from the *Extreme Makeover: Home Edition* program, getting around the house we've always lived in was pretty tough for Patrick Henry. Our old home was small and crowded, with narrow doorframes and hallways, and was not built to accommodate a wheelchair—not even close. Here's what a morning was like for Patrick Henry for nearly twenty years.

When he woke up, he could move himself from the bed to his wheelchair. Getting this done takes several efforts: From the bed, he pulls his wheelchair toward him and locks the wheels. Next, he rolls over on his belly and scoots his way back, feet first. His legs fall over the edge of the bed, and he can place his feet into the footrests. Now he has to push hard to move his upper body—throwing himself backward and getting his bottom onto the edge of the seat. Next, he grabs on to the armrests and supports his weight with his arms, which allows him to slide his bottom fully onto the seat. He has perfected this technique over the years and can do it with surprising quickness.

Unfortunately, once he was in the chair, that's typically as far as he'd get. Even though our house was only one story, it was not handicapped accessible. Consequently, it was extremely difficult for Patrick Henry to maneuver around and get very far in any reasonable length of time. So, each morning, Patricia would help him to the bathroom, then to the kitchen for a bite to eat, then to the family room and the piano. He was always anxious to get to his piano and practice.

After Patricia took Patrick Henry to his piano, she then had to take off and transport Jesse and Cameron to school. I'd still be sleeping, hopefully, trying to get a few extra minutes before starting a long day. That meant if Patrick Henry needed to go back to his room or anywhere else, he was on his own. If it were an emergency, he could, of course, call me to wake me up. But he knew how important any little bit of sleep was to me, and he'd rarely do that. At times, he was amazing—even though he had to go to the bathroom, he'd hold it rather than wake me ahead of schedule. When I finally showed up at the piano, by his reaction, you'd think he hadn't been waiting at all.

If Patrick Henry wanted to maneuver from the family room to his bedroom or the bathroom by himself, this is what he faced. Because he can't fully extend his arms, he can't push both wheels on his chair at the same time. He can push only one or the other, which causes him to zigzag three or four inches one way, then the other, bumping into walls and furniture, trying to assess where he is in the room. Navigating just a few feet in this way takes several minutes.

When he got to the rug in the dining room, it gave resistance and often stopped him in his tracks, bunching up if his wheels didn't hit it just right. If not the rug, sometimes a carelessly placed shoe, pillow, or toy would be an insurmountable roadblock. Due to the rods in his back, Patrick Henry can't lean forward to move things aside. If necessary, he could lock the wheels on his chair, climb down, remove the obstacle, and climb back up. But that takes a lot of effort. When you consider what else awaited him on this journey, he was likely to just stop and stay put.

Why not turn around, if he encountered an obstacle? Unfortunately, turning around was nearly impossible in such close quarters. He was stranded in no-man's-land, away from his piano, but far short of his destination. I know it bugged him, but would he call for me? Nope. He'd let me sleep. When I'd arrive sometime later, I might say, "Hung up on a shoe, huh?" And he'd smile and say, "Yeah, that darn shoe, stealing my time again." No big deal.

If Patrick Henry successfully got over the rug and through the maze of furniture and items left on the floor, the worst was yet to come. He had to make it up the small ramp that leads from the family room to the kitchen. He doesn't have the strength to push his wheels up the ramp, so he'd slide out of his chair onto the floor, careful to keep his chair at arms' reach. Then he'd start crawling on his belly up the ramp while pulling his chair behind him. Actually, he can't really crawl, because he doesn't have the function in his hips and legs, so he had to do a sort of belly-flop, moving forward inches at a time. Finally, in the kitchen, he would begin the climb from the floor to his wheelchair. It's exhausting work.

Back in his chair, he headed toward his bedroom or the bathroom, but that wasn't easy, either. When the old house settled, the floor in our hallway slanted to one side. No problem for most people, but this caused Patrick Henry's wheelchair to go with gravity. It would roll into the wall unless he fought to stop it, which required relentless effort as he moved down the hallway. Next, he would encounter a narrow door jamb. Again, he had to move one wheel at a time, zigzagging, hitting one side of the jamb and then the other, until he finally passed through.

Imagine, you are sitting there at the piano and you decide you want to use the bathroom. Or get a glass of water, put on a sweatshirt, answer the phone, or any of the constant things we run around to do. You or I would take care of what we needed and get back to the piano. Total elapsed time, just a few minutes. When Patrick Henry confronted doing exactly the same thing—this journey of about thirty-five feet—it could take him as long as thirty minutes, provided he could get there at all. And once in the bathroom, it was a whole new Herculean endeavor to move himself from his wheelchair over to the commode, back to the chair and to the sink, manipulate the spigot, reach the soap, wash his hands, and maneuver his chair to fetch a towel.

But when it comes to these struggles, he feels the same way as you or I would about our everyday life activities. He doesn't give them a second thought. "It's normal, just the way things are," he'll shrug.

We live in our new *Extreme Makeover* home now, and its handicapped-accessible construction accommodates Patrick Henry's wheelchair and helps make his life easier in many ways. Even so, many daily tasks are still a struggle, and my son displays a level of courage that is impossible to grasp without seeing it firsthand. I'm blessed to be there with him every step of the way. I can honestly say Patrick Henry's "no big deal" attitude has taught me more about how life ought to be lived than what I learned from all my former teachers and mentors combined.

PATRICK HENRY

My dad talks a lot about how difficult it was for me to move around our old house and how proud of me he was for never giving up. Well, I have a confession to make. For a while, I did give up. Finally, I realized that trying isn't enough, unless you are truly making every possible effort.

For months, I tried to make it up the ramp at our old house. I'd do my belly flops and make some progress. Then I'd either lose my grip on the wheelchair and it would slide back to the bottom, or I'd give out from exhaustion. After a while, I convinced myself that I just couldn't make it, no matter what. But I didn't want my parents to know I believed this, so I showed them that I was still trying, going partway up and then stopping. The truth is, I was just going through the motions.

Then my parents got me the digital cable package for the TV in my bedroom, and that opened up a lot of new TV channels. I like to channel surf, and I discovered that one of those channels showed my favorite game shows in the morning. Suddenly, I was highly motivated to get back to my bedroom before Dad got up. Miraculously, the first time I tried to scale the ramp knowing what awaited me on TV, I was successful. That taught me a lot. Since then, whenever I feel like I'm stuck, I ask myself if I'm really trying as hard as I can.

Some might think that because I have physical challenges, I was a perfect kid, never misbehaving. But I had my ways.

When I was young, sometimes I'd have trouble falling asleep. So I would lie in bed, yelling that I wanted to listen to another tape. Like most little kids, if I didn't get my way, I'd whine and carry on, but Mom wouldn't put up with it. She'd let you know by the tone of her voice when you were getting close to her last nerve.

One night, she got so frustrated with me she called Granddaddy and woke him up so that he would tell me to go to sleep. And I'm sure I did. If Granddaddy told you to do something, you did it.

I was a risk taker, always exploring as much as I could to see what my limits were. One day, while taking a bath, Mom left me alone for a little bit, so I decided to experiment and crawled up on the edge of the tub, then started hanging over, holding on with just one hand. I was doing fine until I hit a slippery spot and fell. Mom came rushing in and there I was, on the floor with a banged-up head. I've never seen one of her looks, but I've heard about them. Dad says they'll freeze you right in your tracks. I'm sure I got one of those looks that day.

She never said it, but I think Mom liked that I would take chances, though I know she didn't want me falling on my head too often. I remember when my little brother, Jesse, was a toddler and learning to walk. I liked to sit on the coffee table in the living room with my feet dangling over the edge. Jesse would crawl over, grab the coffee table, and pull himself up to a standing position. He'd bob up and down several times as if preparing himself for a great feat. Then he'd leap backward, landing on his butt on the floor and laughing hysterically. When Mom told me why he was laughing, it sounded like fun, so I bounced a few times on the coffee table, too, then threw myself backward, body-slamming myself pretty hard on the floor. More ice for my head, but it didn't stop me. After that, knowing that I was going to keep trying to imitate Jesse's jumping, Mom would take pillows off the couch and put them all around the coffee table to soften my landings.

Jesse and I are close in age, just two and a half years apart, so over the years, we played around a lot. When we go swimming, we wrestle in the water and try to dunk each other. We play tag games, like Marco Polo, and I can get around pretty well in the water, so I can go after him. Jesse will come into my bedroom when I'm lying on my bed and jump on me, trying to pin me like in professional wrestling. I'll fight him off. We always razz each other and call each other names, but it's all in fun.

Jesse's into sports. I don't go to his baseball games, because I find them boring. He feels the same way about heading to one of my concerts. But we do have places where my interest in music and his love of sports intersect. When I sing the national anthem before the Louisville Bats baseball game, the Derby Classic basketball game, or the Louisville Fire arena-football game, Jesse is sure to be there.

My brother Cameron is seven years younger than I am. He likes to play guitar, but his taste in music—seventies rock—is different from mine. Like many brothers further apart in age, we love each other and support one another when necessary, but otherwise, we leave each other alone to do our own thing. I think that when he gets older, we'll be closer and will probably find that we have a lot more in common than we think right now, especially when it comes to music.

DAD

Patricia and I wanted Patrick Henry to be as much like other boys as possible, to be daring, because that's the way life is. But it took a while for my wife to get completely comfortable with the idea, because while she wanted him to take chances, she didn't want him taking the lumps that come along with it.

Some children naturally take more risks than others do. We were concerned that because of his physical condition, Patrick Henry might be overly cautious, even scared to do much of anything. We needn't have worried. My son is much more courageous than I ever was as a child. He takes his lumps in stride, sometimes amazingly so. I used to call him Mr. Timex—he takes a licking and keeps on ticking.

Some of his falls were more cute than anything else. When he was around three years old, he had a habit of asking questions he wanted us to ask him. He'd say things like, "Do you want to have some ice cream?" or, because he liked to visit doctors, "Do you want to go to the doctor?" One day, Patricia was taking home movies of Jesse, who was then just a baby, and Patrick Henry was in the background, doing his thing, hanging upside down from the sofa. We were used to this by now and weren't paying attention to him. Then he said, "Are you stuck?" It was obvious he couldn't get himself upright again. Patricia kept filming and turned the camera on him.

"Are you stuck?" he said again, and it looked as if he might fall. Patricia started toward him to bail him out. He was only inches off the floor, and before she could stop him, he plopped down from the sofa onto his head and flopped over to one side. We laughed when we heard him say, "You fell off the couch." Patrick Henry, of course, was fine, but it made the point—he had to be encouraged to take chances, but he also had to know that when he did take chances, it could have consequences.

I would be remiss if I didn't mention the other heroes who share our home and make life worth living. Patricia, as you know, is the unsung hero. She was so instrumental in helping young Patrick Henry forge ahead with his life, while at the same time single-handedly holding our family together. She did this in spite of me and my ignorance of what was required of me; she did it all back then and still does it all today. She is the ultimate mother to her children and complete partner to her husband.

Typical of brothers close in age, Jesse and Patrick Henry are competitive, but in their own unique ways. Jesse will find his way to his older brother's room often enough to let him know he has a pesky younger brother who delights in bugging him. If Patrick Henry ever began developing delusions of grandeur, Jesse would be the perfect antidote. Jesse often is quoted as telling his older brother that the world does not revolve around him, contrary to all the attention and publicity focused on Patrick Henry these days.

Jesse and Patrick Henry will toss barbs back and forth as

brothers do, meant to show one-upmanship and who can get the best of who. But Jesse doesn't push it too hard. He has a big heart, but tries not to show it, and I'm sure he wouldn't want that news to get out to the world—especially to his older brother. In fact, when Jesse does something that needs to be done for Patrick Henry and is helpful, he's quick to say, "Don't think I'm doing this because I love you," or words to that effect. Actually, that's exactly why he's doing it. I've noticed that if I'm distracted or preoccupied, Jesse will get the sense that his older brother might be vulnerable, and he steps right in as his protector. It's touching to watch.

Jesse has played a much bigger role in the success of our family than he realizes. He is self-sufficient in many ways, is an honest, moral young man, gets his homework done without a hassle, helps around the house, and more. All of that is good stuff, but more important than what he does is his attitude about his home life. He knows we have to do many things for and with his older brother—things that take time away from him—and he accepts it with grace.

I've never seen a hint of jealousy from Jesse when it comes to Patrick Henry. That, I'm happy to say, works both ways. Jesse is a fine athlete. When he was in little league, he was a superstar, pitching shutouts, hitting long home runs, you name it. I loved it, and as you know, this was a huge part of my fantasy world when I contemplated having children. But Jesse tends to downplay his triumphs, not wanting the spotlight. He gets that from his mother. Patrick Henry was aware of the immense pride I felt when Jesse hit one out of the park or accomplished any of a dozen other sports heroics. But

Patrick Henry was fine with it. I guess you could say both my elder sons allowed their mother and me to do what we believed was best without our having to worry about how they felt about it.

Cameron, our youngest, is more like me. He loves the limelight and is good at capturing it. He has the timing of a professional stand-up comedian. When put on the spot or asked an absurd question, he's always ready with the most amazing comebacks. One time after an appearance in Louisville, Cameron was standing there with Patrick Henry and me. Folks were asking questions, and one lady said to Cameron, "How does it feel knowing you have a brother that is becoming so famous?" Without blinking an eye, Cameron turned toward Patrick Henry, placed a hand on his shoulder, smiled at him, and asked him, "Yeah, I've been meaning to ask you, how *does* it feel?"

Like Jesse, Cameron does his own thing most of the time. And like Jesse and the rest of us, he is willing to be a role player to make our family work, often showing maturity well beyond his years. He does this even though he is the youngest child, a position that often inspires a taking attitude, rather than a giving one. In that regard, he is not like me, the youngest child in my family, and I'm blessed to be able to say this.

Heroes abound in the Hughes household, each with a unique specialty, and all are critically important to the success of our family.

Patrick Henry has an unusual power to move people to where they want and need to be. Not as a guide or an instructor, but as a subconscious catalyst—that's the wonder of it. Two prime examples are me and my father, Patrick Henry's granddaddy.

I was the youngest of five children, and although I thought my father was a very strict disciplinarian, my siblings tell me I have no idea how strict he was. They tell me he had mellowed quite a bit by the time I came along, but I sure couldn't vouch for that. He'd be quick to let you have it. When I'd invite my friends over to play, they'd always ask if my father was home. If so, they wanted to go somewhere else. You never knew when you might do something wrong without meaning to. My dad worked the night shift and had to sleep during the day. So the worst thing possible was if we might make a noise or drop something and wake him up. We children walked on eggshells when my father was home.

Unfortunately, as I got older, my relationship with my father didn't improve. If anything, it got worse.

I was interested in music ever since I was about seven years old, and I dreamed about making it big, playing to thousands of cheering fans. I loved music so much that after graduating from high school, I majored in it at the University of Louisville. Some music majors intend to do something realistic with their degree, like teach. But my emphasis was on performance, and I saw myself making it as a violinist or pianist, maybe a pop musician, or a member of a city orchestra. I had to rule out major league baseball player years ago, when I realized I couldn't hit the curve ball.

I was pretty serious about my studies until I got my own apartment, at which point things began to slide. Up till then, my father had been paying the bills, so I had to play by his rules. But when I got out on my own, it was a whole different world. My study time dropped off in favor of partying and imbibing a little more than I should have. Things went downhill from there, and after a while, I quit school.

My father was disappointed that I didn't finish college, but then, he always seemed disappointed in me for one reason or another. This time, it was my wasted potential. In high school, I had auditioned and won scholarships to two universities, the University of Louisville and the University of Cincinnati; both scholarships were in the school of music for the violin. My father placed a high value on an education. When he was younger, he really wanted to go to college, working after school and on weekends. He gave the money to his mother to save for him, for his education. But when he got out of high school, he found out the money had been spent and there wasn't any left for college. That must have stung him badly.

After a friend of mine graduated from college, his dad and mine were talking. I was nearby eavesdropping. When the topic of his graduation came up, my dad said, "Boy, it sure must make you proud of him, doesn't it." I longed to hear something like that from my father about me. All of us children were afraid of my dad, but my older brother, Joe, used to fight bitterly with him. They were both alike, and they even looked alike. My father and Joe had thick, dark hair, while the rest of us are fair skinned with blondish hair. Joe was a hell-raiser whom my dad tried to tame, but couldn't.

One night, Joe was out partying late. He was on his way home when a drunk driver found his way onto the expressway going in the wrong direction. Joe tried to avoid him as best as he could, but a big truck on one side and a guardrail on the other penned him in. The drunk driver plowed into him, killing him instantly. Joe was twenty-eight years old; I was twenty-one. My dad never said much about it, but I have a feeling he relived his squabbles with Joe every day after that. It ate him up inside.

My father and I had very different personalities, though as the years passed, we were alike in knowing that our lives weren't what we wanted and that we somehow needed to change. But we were lost as to how to bring about the change. Enter my son and his ability to love completely and without judgment. When you know you aren't living right, you also know that in many ways, you aren't very lovable. So you develop a thick skin that protects you from the assaults you expect to be coming your way. You expect judgment from others and rationalize it. My father and I were great at that.

Patrick Henry showed us we didn't need our armor. His innocence caught us off guard; he accepted us as we were with this pure brand of love that we had never seen or felt before. When you experience this, you can begin the process of rebuilding yourself, because you aren't putting all your energy into defending who you are now.

As much change as I have experienced, my father was changed tenfold.

After Patrick Henry was born, we confronted a problem when Patricia needed to return to work. She had called a number of day-care centers near our home, but was disappointed at their lack of enthusiasm for enrolling a blind child. Thankfully, my mother saved the day and took over. Soon after, my father announced that he intended to retire from General Electric and help care for his grandson. I watched as he and my mother lavished time and attention on him, singing nursery rhymes, reading to him, taking him for walks, eating ice cream. They fed and changed him, put his braces on and took them off, stretched his limbs, massaged his joints. This arrangement when Patrick Henry was so young was a thousand times better than any day-care center. It was also the perfect crucible for my father.

We know grandchildren can bring out the best in their grandparents. But Patrick Henry touched my father in places I didn't know existed. This man was no longer the threatening adult I knew as a child, but a caring, loving marshmallow. It was wonderful to watch, though bittersweet, too. My father died last year, and I'm sure he would have liked to let that other side of him show earlier, but he didn't know how.

The first time I ever heard my father say "I love you" was to Patrick Henry.

PATRICK HENRY

Granddaddy was a prolific reader, always interested in history and particularly war, generals, and famous battles. He had so many books, his living room was completely surrounded by bookshelves to house them all. Late in life, the early stages of Alzheimer's began setting in. Looking back, Dad thinks the first sign was when Granddaddy stopped reading. When Granny asked why he wasn't reading anymore, he said it was because he was tired of rereading the same page.

When Granddaddy was in the later stages of Alzheimer's and had to be moved to a nursing home, I wanted to visit him every day. I really missed him. As the disease advanced, it took a while for him to recognize me and for us to reconnect. But until near the end, he always did, and then it would be just like old times. Weird, but a lot of times, he wouldn't recognize Dad. He'd say Dad was "Dofloppy," the guy who brings his grandson to visit.

Eventually, Granddaddy treated me like a stranger, too, and that was tough. But I knew it wasn't his fault, and I'd always want to go back and try visiting again. People think I have it rough—no way. They should have known Granddaddy before he was sick and then afterward. If they did, they'd realize not only how much he went through, but how much he lost. I still had all our great memories. It broke my heart that he no longer could remember all the things that made life so good.

When you are as close to someone as I was to him, you never want to see that person go, no matter what. But when Granddaddy passed away, I knew it was a blessing that he was back with God. He wouldn't be alone anymore; he would be able to know once again just how much we loved him.

The Best Personal Heroes
Can Be Found Close to Home

PATRICK HENRY

True heroes aren't always easy to spot. Many of us could probably rise to some catastrophic occasion if we were in the right place at the right time. Or, we look to actors and athletes as role models because of how well they can perform. But I believe the greatest acts of heroism aren't necessarily the big attention-getting ones. Instead, they are the smallest: tackling the challenges we face every day with a loving attitude.

We tend to overlook and take for granted the people closest to us, those who do so much and give so unselfishly. But it's time we acknowledged the true heroes in our lives, the ones who don't receive accolades. For me, that means honoring my family and especially my father. Putting your career aspirations and personal goals on hold, binding yourself totally to someone else's schedule, focusing on another's needs while ignoring your own, doing it all on half the sleep you know you need, and doing it every day—that's heroism. My father's example inspires me to be everything I can be.

Do you have a personal hero who goes unrecognized? Why not say thank you today to someone else who has played, or is now playing, a critical role in your life. After all, what would your life be like without this hero?

Are you a personal hero to someone? It doesn't take much. It could be a teacher who has kind words for a struggling student, or a doctor who spends extra time with a frightened patient. Never underestimate the importance of caring and compassion, or the power of small acts of kindness to change someone's life to a much larger extent than you can imagine.

Being a hero to someone is about giving, but don't think it's only a one-way street. When you "do unto others," what you've done will come back to you with dividends somewhere down the road.

Chapter 6

Set Your Course,
Then Burn the Map

Do not turn from it to the right or to the left,
that you may be successful wherever you go.

—JOSHUA 1:7

PATRICK HENRY

Despite some moments of frustration, I've always had the attitude that I could do anything I set my mind to, as long as I gave it my best effort, kept at it and didn't quit.

When I was younger, I said this out loud once. A kid said back to me, "Oh, yeah? If you can do anything you set your mind to, why can't you walk or see?"

I thought about that for a minute and asked him, "Can you do anything you set your mind to?"

"Sure," he said.

"Then why can't you fly or bust through walls like Superman?"

He didn't know what to say.

137

I have my limitations. Everyone does, but the important thing is to figure out what your *true* limitations are. How? You can't know until you keep on trying to reach past them. My parents taught me to go for what I initially think of as being impossible. You may not touch the stars, but you'll know how close you can get. And once you know this, you won't allow yourself to settle for less.

When I was younger, I had a goal, and to reach that goal, I had to become a member of a marching band. When you stop to think about that, it might sound like the dumbest idea ever. I'm blind, I can't walk, and I can't use my arms the way others do. So, how in the world could I march in a band? Here's how it worked out.

I was going to Atherton High School and wanted to take Concert Band as an elective. But there was a problem. To qualify, I had to be in the school's marching band. Not everybody wants to be in the marching band, because it's a lot of hard work. In my case, the difficulty was obvious. The band director's solution was to include me as a member but not as a full participant. When the band practiced drills, since I was in a wheelchair and couldn't see where everyone was going, I wouldn't be out there with the rest of the band on the field. So, I just sat on the sidelines and chipped in by playing my trumpet when I was supposed to.

Originally, I really wanted to play the drums. I love the sound percussion instruments make, the vibrations and the deep, rich tones. But there were problems. I couldn't work the pedals with my feet for the bass drum, or the high-hat cymbals. Nor could I move my body fast enough to hit all the drums in succession, so I had to accept that I wasn't meant to be a drummer.

The trumpet was my second choice. My arms and hands can hold the trumpet and press the valves without a problem, so I took it up and intended to be as good as I could be. As with any instrument, there was a learning curve to forming the right notes and the correct finger combinations. But because I had so much experience playing the piano, I picked up the trumpet pretty quickly, and the band director always praised me for getting my cues right.

At first, getting the breathing pattern down was a little rough because I can't stand up. To get the best sound out of your trumpet, you need full, deep breaths. But I learned to compensate. The only complication I had was when we'd play something like Dixieland music, in which the trumpeters have to put their hands in the bell of the trumpet to change the sound. I can't extend my arms far enough to do that.

At the football games, I sat in the stands with the band until it was time to perform at halftime. Dad would push me out to about midfield and leave me just outside the out-of-bounds line. If someone else couldn't participate because of a sprained ankle or another reason for crutches, he or she would be next to me. The kettle drums were there with me, too, which I was glad about. I wasn't totally off alone on an island.

I didn't particularly want to be in the marching band, but I had to do that to get to my goal, and so I was okay with the whole thing. On the plus side, I escaped the grueling preseason practices that the other band members complained about. In these sessions, you learn how to move quickly through the formations. To hear the band members talk, those practices were as hard as any athletic practice, even football, especially in the late summer, when it's hot and humid. On most days, I could just go home and practice my music in the air-conditioning.

As I got more involved in the season, I enjoyed that I was doing something important with my classmates, even though my participation was different from theirs. I wanted them to know I was just a regular guy like them. I didn't want anyone feeling sorry for me. But as much as this meant, I still knew I wasn't really one of them, a full-fledged band member. I was on the field, but I was "special," and I didn't want to be thought of that way.

When I graduated from high school, I decided to attend the University of Louisville. I thought it would be cool to join the pep band, and Dad, of course, wanted me to be in it, because you get to go to all the home basketball games. Because U of L has a history of successful basketball teams, the arena is always sold out. If you are lucky enough to get a ticket, you can be among the nineteen thousand crazies cheering the team on.

But if you are in the pep band, you are guaranteed a prime seat, every game. If things are going really well with the team, it's possible you could get to go to things like the NCAA tournament or even the Final Four. I'm not a big basketball fan (it's hard for me to follow the games), but Dad is, so I wanted to join not just for me but for him.

I guess I wasn't paying close enough attention when Dr. Greg Byrne, the band director at the University of Louisville, came to my high school to recruit when I was a senior. I got so caught up in the details about pep band I missed what Dr. Byrne was saying about the marching band. Specifically, the "mandatory" part.

When I told Dad about Dr. Byrne's visit, Dad asked me if marching band had to be part of the deal, too, the way it was in high school. I wasn't sure, so Dad called him to find out. Dr. Byrne remembered who I was. He told Dad I had to be a member of the marching band first, *then* I would be eligible for the pep band. Dad said this was fine and then explained to Dr. Byrne what I did in high school—no marching practices and, during the games, sitting on the sidelines—was this what Dr. Byrne had in mind?

It wasn't. Dr. Byrne told Dad I had to be more than a marching band member in name only.

Listening to Dad talk on the phone, I could tell he was starting to heat up by the tone of his voice. He did everything but blurt out, "You idiot, can't you see that he's blind and in a wheelchair?" I sat there thinking, be *in* the band? Is this a joke? Dr. Byrne didn't budge.

"You can't experience the roller coaster by sitting next to it," Dr. Byrne said. "You have to ride it." He told Dad he'd do everything he could to make it work, including making arrangements to have someone push me around the field when the band marched.

When Dad hung up, we talked about what Dr. Byrne had said. I had mixed feelings about it. On the one hand, it would give me the chance to truly be one of the team. But on the other, when I'm in my chair, that's two hundred pounds to push around, and there could easily be a disaster if someone wasn't paying close attention every second. I figured that's what Dad was thinking, and I was right.

Dad didn't go for the idea of turning me over to someone else, because he thought too many things could go wrong. That's when he decided there had to be some way out of this. He intended to call the dean or someone else in the university administration—even the president—to get me out of being a marching band member. Mom laughs about it now and says it was a case of the irresistible force, Dad, meeting the immovable object, Dr. Byrne.

DAD

To say that I was upset by the conversation would be a gross understatement. Throughout Patrick Henry's life, it seemed everyone we met was sympathetic to what he had to contend with, and people always seemed willing to try to help, to accommodate us in any way they could. This was the first time

I encountered someone who intentionally threw up a road-block that seemed unreasonable.

I cooled off after my talk with Dr. Byrne and never did do anything like call the dean. The more I thought about it, the more I felt this whole thing would blow over and work out for us. It always did.

Patrick Henry enrolled at U of L, and I took him to register. We met first with his adviser from the Modern Languages Department, because Patrick Henry was going to be a Spanish major. Next, we went to talk to Dr. Byrne. On the way in, I was ready for a confrontation. I wanted to settle this issue and get my son in the pep band, then make some reasonable arrangements about the marching band. I told myself I wouldn't raise my voice, but that's about the only thing I could guarantee at that point.

Dr. Byrne was sitting behind his desk, looking professorial in his shirt and tie, pen in hand. "Please come in," he waved.

I was surprised. We met, but there was no angry confrontation. On the contrary, Dr. Byrne impressed me with his sincerity. Here was a guy willing to do everything in his power to give each of his students the best experience possible. Dr. Byrne eloquently explained his philosophy of "educational integration"—how learning to coordinate with hundreds of band members who must react as one as they perform complex, intricate maneuvers was a great learning experience that would carry over to many other areas of life. I had to give him credit; he was prepared to act on his word and make any accommodations necessary for any student to get the job done. That included my son.

I listened as Dr. Byrne again offered to have someone else push Patrick Henry around the field. I politely declined the offer.

"I don't think so," I said, shaking my head. "What if they slipped, or rolled into someone? He might even fall out and get hurt if they weren't extra careful every second." My son could be humiliated in front of fifty thousand fans if something went wrong. I couldn't leave him to a stranger.

Dr. Byrne studied me across the desk. "Of course, I understand your concerns," he said. "If Patrick Henry was my son, I'd feel the same way."

Then he smiled. "What about you?"

Okay, so the guy's sincere and charming, I thought. *But I don't think that at my age, I need to be integrated into anything, especially if it means band practice on a field for hours.* I didn't have any time as it was. What about Patrick Henry? As much as he might benefit from such an experience, I was skeptical that it was worth the amount of effort it would require from both of us. And as badly as I wanted my son to be in the pep band, this was getting to be a hassle I didn't need.

Unfortunately, my stance on the matter seemed to be shooting down all our options. This included my calling the university president and raising hell, because I liked Dr. Byrne and didn't want to go there. So I pretended to compromise.

"Okay," I said. "We'll give it a try and see how it goes." We'd go to band camp the first day. Secretly, I was hoping to see if there was one last-gasp angle we could work out. I'd push my son around a bit, thinking that since Dr. Byrne is the kind of guy who seemed to really care about people, maybe when he saw what a burden this would be to us, he'd back down and give us a free pass. Our showing up and giving a good faith effort might just be enough to tug on his heartstrings.

PATRICK HENRY

We arrived at band camp at the university a little before eight in the morning. It was already getting hot, and with the high humidity, the air would soon be thick and steamy. As we got out of the van, Dad commented on the TV panel trucks parked near the entrance. Must be typical preseason coverage, we decided. All things associated with University of Louisville football, even the band, had become big news in town in recent years. Dad moved me to my chair and we started toward the field.

DAD

When we got to the field, the camera crews were milling around, waiting for something to happen. I noticed they perked up when we came by. Patrick Henry was already somewhat well known in the Louisville area. Had word gotten out that he was going to be in the University of Louisville marching band? Not looking back in their direction, I said a quick prayer that they'd vamoose.

Patrick Henry was given a position among the trumpets. I felt conspicuous as all get-out, standing there behind my son in a wheelchair along with more than two hundred students less than half my age. The trumpets were split into three sections of about eight members each. Each section had a leader, an upperclassman who helps organize the section and gives the movement commands during practice.

We started with rudimentary commands. Forward march on the count of four: "One, two, ready, go!" Then we'd march in place—mark time—to a four count before stepping forward sixteen paces. We'd again mark time to a four count, then retreat backward sixteen paces. The seasoned band members knew exactly what to do. We freshmen had a rough time keeping up, and I was the worst of the bunch.

Following orders while pushing the chair was challenging, but the marching band practice field made things a hundred times worse. The field was a mess, nothing like the smooth, grassy surface of the football practice fields. The drainage was terrible, and there were sections with soupy mud, deep ruts, and standing water, perfect for the breeding of mosquitoes. Even though I wouldn't be here more than a day, I felt that the band of a major university in the Big East conference should have far better training facilities than this.

I would have had a tough time pushing the wheelchair even if the field had been pristine, but the sorry condition made it virtually impossible. The small front wheels are meant for hard, predictable surfaces, like concrete and asphalt. Not grass, and especially not mud. Each time I tried to push forward, the small wheels got stuck. This threw me out of step with everyone else, which helped me stand out even more. After a while, I realized if I wanted to move forward, I'd have to lean Patrick Henry backward and push him as though he were doing a wheelie. Going backward wasn't as much of a problem, because the big wheels on the back of the chair were going first.

At this point, my goal was to get through the day without overly burdening the other band members or disrupting what they were trying to do. I worried constantly that I might plow into someone up ahead if I couldn't stop fast enough or, when turning, back into someone.

As the hours passed, I grew more frustrated. Luckily, I had been jogging several days a week and playing a lot of golf, so I was in pretty good shape. But leaning back with the wheelchair while pushing forward for a full day was a very different kind of exercise, and it was tough on my lower back, which was now starting to ache. By afternoon, the field had deteriorated even more. Soon there were places I couldn't take the wheelchair at all. I'd have to scoot Patrick Henry over to the sidelines to get him out of the way, then run back and jump into the formation and keep going.

The worst part was the sun. I had a big sun hat for Patrick Henry and had put sunblock on his face. He had worn long sleeves and pants to protect his arms and legs, but the clothing must have made him feel hotter than blazes. I wore a golf shirt and shorts, and only a little sunblock on my face. When we'd stop, I'd quickly move to shield him from the sun, facing him with my back to the sun. This helped him, but it kept me exposed. By the end of the day, the backs of my arms, neck, and knees were severely sunburned.

Band training camp goes from eight in the morning until eight at night. It was exhausting, and I resolved to make an appointment with the president of the university the next day. Dr. Byrne is a nice guy, and I didn't want to cause him any trouble, but this was ridiculous. I took a breath and looked around. Thankfully, at least the TV camera crews were gone.

Finally, practice was over and we dragged ourselves to the van. Patrick Henry, as usual, seemed in good spirits and no worse for wear. I was completely spent. Knowing I had to be at work at eleven that night didn't help matters.

We got home and cleaned up. A cold shower never felt so good, especially on my sunburned legs. Patricia had something for us to eat, and since I hadn't eaten much of anything earlier because I was so hot and miserable, I devoured dinner. While we ate, Patricia tried to comfort me. Looking at me sunburned and all bent over, she was probably worried that doing this every day might kill me.

After eating, I turned on the TV to catch some of the news, as I normally do before leaving for work. I couldn't believe what I saw.

The teaser was a shot of me pushing Patrick Henry around the practice field and how wonderful I was to be doing that to give my son the chance to participate. The other local news channels led off with our story, too. My jaw dropped. With this on the air, I was toast. Everything pointed toward my continuing with band camp for another nine days.

The deal was cemented when the e-mails and phone calls started pouring in, congratulating me for being so giving and loving. But all I could think about was how tomorrow would be another day of pushing and pulling Patrick Henry through the mud and ruts, fighting off mosquitoes and getting more sunburned. And before I had that pleasure, a shift at UPS was waiting for me. I groaned. Why me, Lord?

PATRICK HENRY

Dad was such a good sport about all this. I didn't even know he got so badly sunburned until now. At the time, he really didn't complain much to me how his body hurt or let on about how much he hated band camp. He just kept going, no matter what.

Folks often want to know how the band members responded to us at the beginning. I worried they'd figure we were trouble. One way to look at it is, if I'm a trombone player and I'm close to that crazy guy and his kid in the wheelchair, I'd better move fast or he might plow into me and break my leg. Or, maybe we might cause a big pileup at midfield, and band members would start falling like dominos.

But in reality, the other band members couldn't have been better about our being there. Dad felt that we were accepted right away, and he's pretty sensitive to those sorts of things, especially where I'm concerned. Early on at band camp, we needed to learn some of the new musical pieces. Most of the time we march to theme music from a popular movie, like *The Incredibles*. Dr. Byrne knew I played by ear, so like Miss Hinda, he recorded some of the music for me and sent it to the house. This allowed me to get familiar with the music ahead of time.

At our first indoor practice, caused by an unexpected rainstorm, there was a music stand set up for me with sheet music on it. As we played, some of the band members around me apparently noticed I wasn't turning the pages. Maybe they thought I couldn't reach the stand because of my arms, so they started reaching over and turning the pages for me. I didn't know this until Dad told me about it later. It was so nice, and it made me feel that much more welcome. I didn't even realize it, but the other members must not have known at first that I was blind. I guess my eyes must look pretty good.

During a performance, there will be times when you have what's called *silent horns up*. This means when everything stops and the band director gives a sign for all horns to be raised silently and in unison. The problem is, I can't see the sign that's given. To help me, the band members, on their own, decided to give a little verbal cue, like a sort of swooning sound, to tell me what's happening. It's not perfectly in keeping with good band decorum, but it works and I definitely appreciated it. When Dr. Byrne saw this gesture, he called it a "God moment." There were a lot of those along the way.

DAD

We went back the next day, and it was more of the same—mud, bugs, and stifling heat. But because I had accepted that this was the way it was going to be, somehow it didn't seem quite as bad. For Patrick Henry's sake, I put on a smile and talked like this was no big deal. "Who knows, I bet something good will come out of this," I'd say. As I liked to tell my sons, when you fall into a big pile of manure, there's got to be a pony somewhere nearby. The problem was, I was looking pretty hard, but there was no pony in sight.

As band camp went along, I got better at moving Patrick Henry around, unless it had rained and the whole field was swampy. The small front wheels on the wheelchair were still a problem, but at least I was beginning to get a feel for where we needed to be on the field, positionwise, and how I was supposed to get there. Following the person in front of you helps (although only until your paths must diverge). I had to be alert constantly. Honestly, I was terrified of making a stupid and dangerous mistake in the future while we performed at halftime, like dumping my son out of his chair onto the ground. Or, if something went wrong and I had to jump out of line for some reason, I knew we'd not only screw up the formation, but also stand out like a red neon sign at midnight. I could handle it, but I didn't want my son to be part of that.

Being modestly successful at tinkering, I decided to try to do something about the front wheels on the wheelchair. I had to do something if I was going to survive another week. The small front wheels pivot easily, which means when they hit an uneven surface, they turn sideways. So, you have to keep pulling back to straighten the wheels before you can move ahead. It was constantly one step forward and two steps back. I knew right away I couldn't keep doing that, and that's why I had to lean Patrick Henry back in his chair, lifting the front wheels off the ground. But that was too grueling, and at my age, I knew my body would be breaking down soon.

I attached a makeshift straight axle—really a long, steel rod threaded like a screw—to the front of the chair. To the axle I attached bigger wheels from Patrick Henry's old red Radio Flyer wagon. This accomplished two things. It locked the front wheels in place, and it raised the front of the chair several inches. But I soon realized there was a trade-off. Because the new, bigger wheels were fixed and wouldn't turn at all, pivoting was a real challenge. On top of this, I had to attach the axle and then remove it after each practice to maneuver again in the real world. The way I had it constructed, these actions added forty minutes on top of everything else. Finally, God sent another angel to save the day.

Dave Fuchs, an expert machinist, was a friend of my best man, Michael Rundell, who asked him to take a look at the wheelchair and see what he might come up with. He came by, looked at my Rube Goldberg setup, and laughed. "I can throw something together for you that might work," he said. And it did.

He figured out how to make the big wheels rotate independently a full 360 degrees, just like the old smaller wheels, and fixed it so the big wheels didn't bump into Patrick

Henry's footrests. What's more, he designed the modification so that by removing one bolt, I could change it out in about five minutes and without getting my hands covered in grease. We tried it in the backyard, and it worked perfectly.

The modified wheelchair notwithstanding, after a week or so of band camp, I was completely exhausted. It wasn't so much from the effort on the field, but from the lack of sleep. I can do okay with about 4-1/2 to 5 hours of sleep per night. But these days, I was getting far less, because we needed to be at the camp before 8:00 A.M. I decided to talk to Dr. Byrne, who understood completely. In fact, he wished I had come to him earlier. He regretted that I had been through so much during that first week. He agreed to let us out of the morning practice session. But we still had to go eight hours, through the hottest part of the day.

PATRICK HENRY

Band camp leads right up to the first football game of the year. The game was one of the biggest, because we were playing our in-state rival, the University of Kentucky, and there would be a huge national audience. Dad was worried sick about all the things that could go wrong. And with two hundred students moving fast in every direction, the odds were pretty good that something would. I could tell in his voice how nervous he was, especially when he learned the cameras would zero in on us during the halftime show. I assured him we'd be great, but Dad worried that since this was our first game ever, he'd choke and do something stupid, like plow into somebody or dump me.

Before the game, the band does a traditional drum-line march around the outside of the stadium, greeting the thousands of tailgaters. When the drummers started, the electricity in the air was amazing. I had big goose bumps, and Dad says his were even bigger, though at that moment, he was bursting with pride to be out there with me. No longer did he feel like a big pothole in the middle of the expressway.

"The band members know exactly what to do," he reminded me. "All we have to do is be on our toes and follow the right people. Luckily, we're going through the easier formations, so we'll be fine." Later, as the season moves along, we learn patterns that are more complicated.

I just nodded my head. "You're right, Dad. We'll be fine."

Of course, Dad had a panic attack when we started into our first formation at halftime. At practice, he had learned everyone else's position and used them as reference points for where we needed to go. He knew that Zack, tall with a beard, would be over to the left, and Joel, stocky with long hair, would be over to the right, and so on. They were familiar faces and bodies, and they worked like a compass. What Dad didn't plan on was that at the game, everyone would be dressed alike in our uniforms and hats. Worse, with our hats on, Dad could see only about four inches of face, not nearly enough for a quick reference. Add to that the university band rule of no facial hair, so all the guys had shaved off their beards and mustaches. It was as if everyone was suddenly camouflaged.

Dr. Byrne had scripted formations and movements to go along with music from the movie *Gladiator*, and some are tricky. At one point, the band splits into two blocks, which march toward each other as though we're going to do battle. When we meet in the middle, we mesh quickly into one big block, then move fast into a diamond shape, and then on to another formation. Dad has to turn me on a dime and speed off in the opposite direction. If his timing is off by even just a few seconds, he might run over one of the trombone players coming to take the spot where he was just standing.

Dad was about to lose it early in the routine when another trumpet member came to the rescue, taking his finger off the trumpet and pointing to where Dad needed to be. Others seemed to know Dad was in trouble, too, and they went out of their way to help. Meanwhile, all I had to do was play the trumpet. It was great.

Fortunately, there was a backup plan. Dr. Byrne had been thinking ahead from the first time he talked with Dad, and he kept us in mind during the early summer as he was scripting the formations and moves for the halftime shows. He realized in the choreography for *Gladiator*, some maneuvers could challenge Dad's ability to react fast enough. Dr. Byrne had worried this might be too much, especially so early in the season. To be able to do many of these moves requires what Dr. Byrne calls muscle memory—your body just knows what to do automatically without the brain intervening. There's no time for thinking, and the moves have to become as natural as reflexes. With this in mind, Dr. Byrne built in an escape plan for me and Dad if we needed it. He put us in a place in the formation that would allow us to duck out gracefully at a critical time, then fit back in a little bit later without anyone really noticing. Pretty cool, and wonderful of him to be concerned about us, even before we became official members of the band. We were both amazed that way back then, our director was so confident this would work out the way it did.

In interviews about our experiences at band camp and later at practices, Dad likes to say, "It's a little bit of a workout, but it's been a lot of fun." When I've heard Dad talk to his friends, he tells a different story. He says band camp was more like football boot camp under legendary coach Paul "Bear" Bryant. When Coach Bryant was at Texas A&M, he worked his players, known as "the Junction Boys," nearly to death in the Texas summer heat, just to see who really wanted to be there and play for him. It was so horrible, he ran most of the players off because they couldn't take it anymore. But the ones who stuck it out won football games. I guess we went through something a little like that, or, I should say, Dad did. But we knew every minute was worth it at the University of Kentucky game when we were out there on the field playing "My Old Kentucky Home."

Once word got out about my participation in the University of Louisville marching band, the publicity began to take on a life of its own, and 2006 turned out to be a pretty incredible year. Dad and I never thought we'd attract so much attention, but we did. One day, Dad got a phone call and we were surprised to learn that I had won the Disney Wide World of Sports Spirit Award. The award is presented each year to "college football's most inspirational person or team." We didn't even know I'd been nominated. The award ceremony was set for December 7 at Disney World. I couldn't wait to go.

"This is bigger than being just about sports, and it's not just about being in the band," Dad told me. "It's more about being a good person, and about courage and the willingness to help others." I liked that, and it made the award even more meaningful to me. But when he told me about some of the past winners, I was amazed and honored to be thought of in the same way.

Past winners included a high school student who had to give up playing football when he donated one of his kidneys to his ailing grandmother. Wow! He was the first one to receive the award in 1996. Another award winner was a young man who had to have his right leg amputated and still managed to play football. What courage it must have taken to even try to play. And the winner in 2002 was, like me, from the University of Louisville. Dewayne White lost both parents, survived two house fires and serious injuries, and went on to star at Louisville, and later as a pro in the NFL.

The award ceremony was wonderful. Dad and I were backstage waiting while they showed a profile of me from ESPN. After the applause, Mr. Kellen Winslow, a former great professional football player, came onstage to introduce us. He's the director of sports for Disney World, which has a huge sports complex and all sorts of activities going on year-round.

As a nonathlete, I didn't meet the typical criteria for the award. But Mr. Winslow told the audience I was starring on the football field, even though I'd never seen a game in my life. He said I practiced as hard as any athlete did, and I wore my uniform with pride—the uniform of the marching band at the University of Louisville. He said he was especially proud to be presenting this award to me, because I was the first ever non–football player to win the Spirit Award. At that point, Dad pushed me onto the stage, and there was applause again.

One thing I really loved about that day was that Dr. Byrne was there with Dad and me. I felt as though he earned a big part of the award and I was glad he was sharing it with us. When they handed me the award, I had a little speech prepared. It wasn't much. First, I thanked God for all my blessings and for the opportunity to be there. I thanked all the folks at Disney for selecting me, and then I thanked my mom, my brothers, my grandparents, Dr. Byrne, and Dad.

But the best part about the ceremony was knowing how much Dad was enjoying it, because he's such a sports nut. Before we went on, he kept telling me, "There's so-and-so," and "Can you believe we're in the same room with this guy or that guy?" I didn't know anything about any of the people he mentioned, and all I knew to say back was, "Awesome!"

DAD

The Disney Wide World of Sports Spirit Award is part of a bigger celebration put on by the National College Football Awards Association, in which twenty-one awards are given out for all sorts of accomplishments in football. It was paradise for sports fans, and I really soaked it up. All the ESPN *College Game Day* football crew were there—Chris Fowler, Lee Corso, and Kirk Herbstreit—as well as current and past award winners in all categories, their coaches, agents, tons of hall-of-famers, and the list goes on.

Seeing all these sports dignitaries under one roof was overwhelming, but the most unbelievable thing of all was that my son was there and was about to be honored by them. The second most amazing thing was sitting down next to Dick Butkus, the greatest linebacker of all time. He was so gracious to us.

Although I know Patrick Henry wasn't nervous, I sure was. This was very heady company we were in, but to my son, we were simply surrounded by a bunch of wonderful human beings, just like everywhere else we go. And you know what? After they showed a profile of Patrick Henry and many of the audience were teary-eyed, I realized that these superhuman, muscular marvels had shown us their most human side. I felt that on this night, in that audience, they knew where he was coming from and they appreciated him all the more for it. They showed us what my son sees in everyone right from the start.

As usual, Patrick Henry was calm and collected, and connected immediately with everyone in the audience. But as much as he was thankful for the award and very appreciative of all that goes with it, I know he was really anxious to get out in the Disney World park and onto Space Mountain.

Dr. Byrne came with us to Disney World for the ceremony. Back then, I didn't know Dr. Byrne well, other than to say hello and make casual conversation. On the flight down, we sat together and had a good talk in which we came to really know one another.

I confided that during our first telephone conversation about Patrick Henry's mandatory participation, I was close to screaming at him. He laughed and told me he thought I was getting a little testy, but he understood why. As an educator, Dr. Byrne had seen many accommodations made for disabled students like my son, but he'd had no idea how much Patrick Henry copes with every day and how much more needed to be done out there in society. "But I never doubted this would work out," he said, still determined to help in any way he could.

As it happened, Dr. Byrne had encountered Patrick Henry once before. Ten years ago, he and his wife were attending the Gaslight Festival in Jeffersontown, a small town east of Louisville. Patrick Henry was ten years old at the time, and he was participating in a parade and playing piano on a float being pulled by a pickup truck. Dr. Byrne had no idea who he was, but in seeing my son for the very first time, he turned to his wife and told her, "Look at that . . . I'd love to have that young man in my band someday." It was as if Dr. Byrne had been in his office all that time, waiting for us to walk through the door.

There are so many coincidences and ironies that some might think we are making them up. Here's another one.

In the beginning, I questioned Dr. Byrne's sanity, and I was determined to do everything in my power to short-circuit what I saw as this marching-band fiasco. If I had been successful, things in my life and in the lives of my family would have gone in a much different direction.

Recently, the Athletic Department at the University of Louisville decided to take over the pep band. When this happened, the department removed participation in the marching band as a prerequisite for pep band.

If this move had taken place a bit earlier, Patrick Henry would have gone straight to the pep band as we had planned, and I would have had my cherished basketball game tickets, tagging along with my son. Life would have been good as far as we could tell. But we would have missed the most important engagement of our lives: the opportunity to slog around on a muddy field with more than two hundred weary marching-band members on hot and humid August afternoons, and everything that followed thereafter.

And now, the ultimate irony. Once the Athletic Department took over, Patrick Henry decided he didn't want to be in the pep band if Dr. Byrne was not going to be associated with it. I supported his decision. So, here we are, full members in the marching band, without participating in the very thing that started us down this road in the first place.

I had resisted mightily. I stomped and yelled and gnashed my teeth. I threatened, pouted, and postured, but thankfully, God pays no attention to such things. Instead, He simply proceeded with His plan for us, and He enlisted Dr. Greg Byrne to put us on the right course.

Set Your Course, Then Burn the Map

PATRICK HENRY

Our goals tell us what we intend to accomplish, and the plans we make are what we believe to be the most effective path. But what if along the way we find that the bridge is out? You may have to accept that your map doesn't match up with the road of real life. At that point, forget the directions and look around for a better route. Keep going, but be smart about it, and that includes being flexible. Quite often, those who achieve great things got there by a route they hadn't planned on, and to do that, you have to be open to all possibilities. Many of the greatest inventions were discovered by accident.

My goal was to be in the pep band and to avoid the marching band. Dad and I set our course accordingly, but God had other plans for us. When it was obvious all roads were leading us to the marching band, we could have forsaken our goal and quit. But I was determined to be in the pep band, so we changed course and embraced the marching band. And when we did, we discovered that the marching band rewarded us in many wonderful ways. God's plan for us was far better than the one we had started with, but we had to be open in order to find that out. Joel Osteen, senior pastor of Lakewood Church in Houston, refers to this as "stumbling into God's blessings."

Life never runs smoothly, and you can bet Murphy's Law will come into play somewhere along the line—whatever can go wrong will. When life is unkind and you're not sure what to do or which way to go, pray about it. Ask God to help you set the best course of action that will help you reach your goal, and once it is set, dedicate your whole being to the process. And when things look their worst, don't look back. Look up instead: Have faith in where you are going and faith in the one who is guiding you. If the bridge is out, ask God for Plan B. He'll have it ready for you.

Chapter 7

Love, Given Freely, Multiplies and Returns

The love of God is greater far,
than tongue or pen can ever tell.
—FREDERICK M. LEHMAN (1868–1953)

PATRICK HENRY

Whenever I couldn't get to my piano, I knew at least I'd always have my voice with me. I think the first thing I ever hummed was the theme to *Jeopardy,* at about age 2-1/2. Since then, my singing has come a long way.

Performing is more to me than sharing a love of music. It's become the way I make friends—if people like what I'm doing, then they might want to come up to meet me. Most musicians connect with an audience with their eyes. I can get a feel for approximately how many people might be out there in a crowd by the applause, the chatter, or the way the sound travels, but that's about it. The best way for me to connect is through touch—shaking your hand, giving a hug, or exchanging a kiss on the cheek—although, of course, I can't do that while I'm playing. I have to wait until afterward. So, I view singing, the piano, and the trumpet as my calling cards. I especially enjoy church performances because there are usually a lot of ladies who will give me kisses.

When people see me sing or perform music for the first time, they often tell me I didn't seem nervous at all. They're usually surprised to hear I've been doing this since I was a little kid. I started performing in public by making appearances with my Dad on the annual Crusade for Children, a telethon to raise money for children's charities and to help kids like me. It's broadcast on WHAS-TV and WHAS (AM) radio in Louisville, and it gave us a lot of exposure in our hometown.

After doing the crusade for a few years, I was invited to appear on *Maury,* a national TV talk show hosted by Maury Povich, when I was almost twelve—an episode called "Incredible Children." Mom, Dad, and I were going to be on with four other kids and their parents. One of the other kids on the show suffered from brittle bone disease. She was really tiny and her life was hard, because the slightest injury could break her bones. I felt bad that she always had to be so careful. She couldn't play around or take any chances, like I do going on rides at amusement parks or wrestling with my brothers. When you see the things that have been taken away from another person, it makes you appreciate the blessings you have.

Back in the green room before we went on the air, Mom and Dad had all kinds of instructions for me. Don't mumble, and be sure to speak up, sit up straight, smile, and be enthusiastic. Then they told me if I did everything the way I was supposed to, they'd treat me to a big piece of New York cheesecake. Dessert is usually a good way to attract my attention. The funny thing is, we forgot we were wired up at the time, and before long, the staff came in with a whole cheesecake for us.

Taping the show was fun. Mom, Dad, and I and Mr. Povich sat around talking for a while, then I played piano and sang "Live, Laugh and Love," a song by Clay Walker. Dad is usually comfortable in front of an audience, since he's a musician, too. Mom gets more anxious, but she always does fine. On this show, it didn't matter. They completely cut out the parts with Mom and Dad and just kept me. Dad joked that they blew his shot at his fifteen minutes of fame.

DAD

I can't remember Patrick Henry ever being nervous before performing. He looked forward to it, and he loved the music so much, he just couldn't wait to get out there. But like any parent, I was often a nervous wreck for him. It was the big finale for the Crusade for Children fund-raising week, and nine-year-old Patrick Henry was going to sing the "Crusade Cannonball." It was a takeoff of the song "Cardinal Cannonball" by local singer and songwriter Mickey Clark, in which he sang about the University of Louisville Cardinals basketball team headed to the NCAA final four.

We put together a whole new set of words and paid tribute to the biggest Crusade donors, companies like Kroger and GE, and made it fun at the same time. I told Patrick Henry I'd be behind the curtain, about eight feet away, if he forgot any of the words. I had a clipboard with all the lyrics, and I couldn't imagine that he'd get through it without my help, all those company names to remember and rhyming them on cue. I was pacing, not knowing what he might do if he got stuck.

Well, I needn't have worried. He sang the whole darned song perfectly, not one misstep. I think that was my proudest moment among many.

At another crusade finale, Patrick Henry, age eleven, was invited to sing a duet with Bryan White, the country music star who was brought to town as a guest celebrity. They sang "From This Moment," a song he made famous with Shania Twain. Patrick Henry was supposed to sing Shania's part. Given Patrick Henry's young age and limitations, perhaps Mr. White didn't really expect my son to hold up his end. When they started singing, Bryan sang right over the top of Patrick Henry, probably thinking he was protecting a boy from being embarrassed. Then my son started belting it out, and Bryan noticed—*Hey, this kid can sing!* After that, Bryan did his part, then waited for Patrick Henry, and they sang a real duet.

PATRICK HENRY

I love all types of music, but the one that has become my favorite is country. The lyrics are clever and the stories are sung from the heart; it's pure American and there's nothing else like it. Mom introduced me to it—she was always listening to WAMZ, the big country station in Louisville. When I was about seven, I heard the radio playing a catchy song, "I Should Have Asked Her Faster," by Ty England. For me, it was love at first listen.

Later, when I really got into country, I wanted to meet some of the singers I was listening to every day, like Patty Loveless, Emmylou Harris, and Tanya Tucker. Dad said we could go to a concert, where I could hear some of the stars from a distance, but I wouldn't be able to actually meet them. So I sat down and wrote to eight of my favorite singers. I sent each of them two versions of a letter: one in Braille, which showed them I was blind, and a regular, typed version they could read.

I told them about myself and how big a fan I was. Mostly, I got autographed pictures back with a short note. This was cool, and Mom put the pictures in frames and hung them in my room. Then one day, as we were on the way home from somewhere, Dad stopped at the mailbox and pulled out a package. It didn't look familiar: It was plain and was addressed to me with no markings or return address. Nobody in my family was expecting anything. Dad opened it slowly, as if making sure it wasn't a bomb.

It was a cassette tape. Since we were still in the car, Dad popped it in the player.

We sat there and listened. It turned out to be a message from country singer Miss Pam Tillis in response to my letter. It was the neatest thing. She said, "Hi, Patrick Henry. I got your letter and just wanted to get back to you. I'm sitting here with my mom on the back porch. It's been raining . . ." Then she talked for about five minutes, asking me how I was doing and other questions about myself. I was in heaven.

If all the country music stars were anything like Miss Tillis, it made me want to meet them even more. But how?

Mom started checking around and discovered an event in Nashville called the Fan Fair. It's a giant concert event at Opryland with hundreds of artists. The stars also have autograph-signing booths, and at certain times during the fair, you can meet them. I was so excited I immediately begged Dad to take me that June. Dad wasn't into country music too much at the time, and I could tell by his hesitant response— he paused and got quiet for a minute—that this was not something he wanted to do. But knowing how badly I wanted to meet my music idols in person, he agreed.

My parents tease me about my "driving things into the ground." Once I knew we were going to Fan Fair, I'd ask them about it every day. Finally the day in June arrived, and Dad and I were off in the van, ready to spend four days in Nashville.

We knew nothing about how the Fan Fair worked, so we bought some tickets and just showed up. We thought getting there at nine in the morning was early, but when we arrived, there were already three hundred people in line to meet Trisha Yearwood, and she wouldn't even be there for another hour. The last guy at the end of the line had a sign that read, "No more tickets." We didn't even know you had to have other tickets once you were inside just to stand in line.

We found out later that folks will line up outside the building as early as four o'clock in the morning just to be the first ones through the main doors when they open. They dash to the booths where tickets are given out, and if the people are among the lucky first three hundred to get tickets for Trisha Yearwood, then they can come back later and line up and wait for her.

Dad was kind of bummed out. He pushed me around the exhibition hall awhile, looking for something that would make my trip worthwhile, but nothing promising appeared. We were on our way to another hall when an official-looking lady stopped us. Dad said she had a badge of some sort around her neck. "How are you liking the Fan Fair?" she asked.

I piped up and said, "I love it!" Dad told her he had hoped I could meet some of the stars, but it wasn't working out.

She asked me who I wanted to meet. "Trisha Yearwood," I said.

I couldn't believe it, but this wonderful woman took me and Dad right to the front of Miss Yearwood's line. I met her, and we even sang a song together, "X's and O's." Her booth was special because it had a soundproof mini-recording studio in it, and if you wanted to, you could sing a few lyrics with her and record a tape they gave you as a souvenir.

The nice woman waited there, and when I was done, she asked if I wanted to meet anyone else. I said, "Sure!" and we made the rounds to booth after booth, meeting the who's who of country music: Lee Ann Rimes, Tim McGraw, Merle Haggard, Naomi Judd, Mark Chestnut, and Martina McBride. It was awesome.

I couldn't wait to go back the next year. Since we couldn't count on a fair official to magically be there to usher us around, Dad found out who was going to be there in advance. We'd try to get there earlier, but I knew there was no way Dad was going to line up in the middle of the night to meet a country singing star.

We arrived at Fan Fair, and like last year, there were long lines zigzagging everywhere. The booths vary in size, but most are about twenty or thirty feet across, with an entrance side and an exit. The "in" line forms on the left. Folks come into the booth one at a time, say hi, get an autograph, and then leave on the opposite side.

Dad figured that if we went to the exit side, we'd be close to the artists and maybe I'd still have a chance to meet them. So we went to the exit side of Miss Pam Tillis's booth and waited. As we waited and the time got close for Miss Tillis to appear, I decided to entertain the crowd by singing some of her songs. The folks in line loved it. Then Miss Tillis came out, saw me singing, and came right over. Dad told her I was the one who had sent her a letter in Braille and that she responded with a wonderful tape. She remembered and was delighted to meet me face to face.

Each year when I'd go back to Fan Fair, I was sure to go to Miss Tillis's booth, where we'd sing one of her songs and talk like old friends. In 2001, after four years of these brief visits, out of the blue she asked me if I'd like to come to the Grand Ole Opry on Saturday night and sing with her. I was in total shock, as were my parents. The Grand Ole Opry! I don't stutter, but I think I did when I answered, "Yes!" On the way back to the hotel, Mom was beyond excited. She told me all about the Opry, and how this was the place all the great stars got their start. The original place was an old Baptist church, with pews and no air-conditioning, but the new one was supposed to be state-of-the-art, and she was anxious to see it. I couldn't wait.

The Opry has two shows, the early one around eight and a later one at about eleven. The first one is local, just for the audience. The later show goes on national TV. The producer said I could go on the early show, but Miss Tillis said she wanted me on both. I don't think too many people say no to Miss Tillis, so I had to get ready for my big debut. She told me we'd sing some of her recent hits, but she wasn't sure exactly which ones. I guess she decides once she's ready to perform and sees what the audience might most want to hear.

Mom said I needed a country-and-western get-up, so we went clothes shopping for jeans and a fancy western shirt. We also had to pick up Miss Tillis's latest CD, because I didn't know the words to all the songs, and if she picked one I didn't know, well, I'd be in trouble. We got back to our hotel room, and I made sure I learned all the lyrics. After the shows, Dad found out that the producers had been concerned about how I'd do on TV, that maybe I'd forget the words, but they'd relaxed when they saw us perform in the earlier show. We had a ball singing together.

Anytime I see Miss Tillis on stage, she has always invited me up to sing with her. On one occasion, I couldn't make it up on the stage, so she brought two microphones down to me, and we sang from the audience. All the country music stars I've met are great, but Miss Tillis is extra nice.

DAD

I never cease to be amazed at the reaction of people to my son. The Nashville stars are busy with packed schedules and people wanting their attention night and day. But when Patrick Henry appears, they drop what they're doing and come right to him as if he's a magnet. It's clear their affection for him is genuine and heartfelt.

I have to admit, I dreaded going to Fan Fair the first time. When I saw the announcement, I wanted to run and hide: "Four days, 30 hours of autograph signing, 100 hours of live music, 400 country music artists and celebrities, and thousands of revved up music lovers all combine to create the ultimate country music fan experience." From the description, the idea struck me as something Dante would cook up. But after getting into it over the years, I have come to enjoy country music and the whole scene very much.

In addition to Pam Tillis, Patrick Henry struck up quick and meaningful relationships with a number of the stars. In 2002, Lane Brody and Patrick Henry became friends when we showed up at her booth and they sang a song together. She invited him to sing with her at a Fan Fair event at Riverfront Stages in Nashville. There were thousands of fans in the crowd, and of all the acts, she and Patrick Henry brought the house down. When Richie McDonald, the lead singer of Lone Star, met Patrick Henry at his booth, he invited us backstage for their performance at the Grand Ole Opry. He and Patrick Henry found a piano and played songs the whole time while they were waiting to perform. Then my son sang the song "No News" with Lone Star on stage. From then on, when we'd visit their booth at Fan Fair, the whole group would come out and gather around Patrick Henry and they'd sing to the crowd.

Patrick Henry

I don't want you to think I've abandoned other types of music in favor of country. I love the blues and jazz piano, like Ray Charles and Duke Ellington. And I enjoy playing themes from Broadway musicals, as well as classic songs like "Paper Moon" and "I Left My Heart in San Francisco." When it comes to music, I'm open-minded and will play just about anything.

Classical music has a special place in my heart, even though, these days, it's not the kind of thing I'll listen to on my headphones for fun. It's more like I have great respect for it and the masters who created it. I appreciate its complexity and how demanding it can be to play. To me, learning classical pieces is the key to getting better on the piano.

It has never been my ambition to be a concert pianist, but

you'd think it was, if you knew my teacher, Miss Hinda Ordman. She loves the classic masters and their music, but she never pushed me in that direction, although I think she felt that I could get there if I really wanted to and if I worked hard enough.

In 2002, I had my first public recital, which took place at the Cathedral of the Assumption in downtown Louisville. It was Miss Hinda's idea, a way to "put me out there" as a performer. She was nervous, and my parents were, too, especially because Mr. Lee Luvisi was in the audience. I didn't know he was there until I had finished.

During my lessons, when we'd take a break, Miss Hinda would tell me about famous musicians like Luvisi. A virtuoso pianist, he made his Carnegie Hall recital debut when he was only twenty years old. After that, he was soloist for just about every important orchestra in North America, and he performed under famous conductors like Leonard Bernstein, William Steinberg, and Eugene Ormandy. And after all that, he came back to his hometown—Louisville—and became Artist in Residence at the University of Louisville School of Music.

It was a Sunday afternoon, and I played for about an hour and a half: two Bach two-part inventions, in F-major and A-minor; a Haydn piano sonata in C-major; Tocatina in A-minor by Dmitri Kabalevsky; Chopin's Minute Waltz and his waltz in C-sharp minor. I finished up with Mozart's twelve variations on the theme *Ah! Vous dirai-je, Maman* ("Twinkle, Twinkle Little Star"). The cathedral was packed, thanks to Dad's beating the bushes and convincing everyone we've ever known to come. Not many folks like classical music, so I'm glad they came to hear me play, and when I finished, they applauded and cheered.

After I played, Mr. Luvisi came up and introduced himself to me. He told me how much he enjoyed my performance and that he was much older than me when he learned Mozart's twelve variations. I didn't know what to say, other than thank you. If Miss Hinda had heard him say this to me, I know what she'd be thinking. Hmmm, if Mr. Luvisi had his Carnegie Hall recital debut at age twenty, and he was older than me when he learned Mozart's variations . . . then maybe I was on track to follow in his footsteps, and maybe even a little ahead of schedule. Ha-ha. But I know Miss Hinda. She always builds me up and tells me I'm great, and I really appreciate her support. But there's only one Lee Luvisi, and I'm glad I got to meet him and that he said such nice things about my playing.

My high point for the piano was May 16, 2005, when I got to perform at the John F. Kennedy Center for the Performing Arts in Washington, D.C. The opportunity came as a result of a contest held by VSA arts of Kentucky (formerly known as Very Special Artists). This nonprofit organization was founded by Jean Kennedy Smith in 1974 to support artists like me who might be physically or mentally challenged. To enter, I had to prepare an audiotape of my music and submit it.

Every state has a VSA arts association, and each has an

annual contest to determine the best performance in visual and audio art. I had competed five years in a row, and had won the State of Kentucky contest each year. The winner of each state is then entered in a national competition. In the fourth year, I came pretty close to winning. Then, on my fifth try, I won.

I was so happy to be chosen, but here's the really cool part. Each year, two VSA arts artists from the United States are selected to appear at the Kennedy Center, along with two artists from foreign countries. Something happened the year I went, because the two foreign artists couldn't make it. So, that gave my U.S. partner and me more time to perform. I selected a variety of pieces, including "Razzle Dazzle," from the stage play *Chicago*, "Rustles of Spring," by Christian Sinding, and, again, Mozart's twelve variations on the theme "Twinkle Twinkle Little Star." Then, my partner, a young lady from Pennsylvania, and I did a piano duet by Gabriel Faure.

The Kennedy Center is a grand place on the banks of the Potomac, near the Lincoln Memorial and not far from the infamous Watergate Hotel. Dad described the concert hall to me: huge crystal chandeliers from Norway and a pipe organ with over four thousand pipes. Imagine! I'd love to hear it sometime. The seating is set up like the great European halls, with more than 2,500 seats, and the sound is incredible, with a fantastic, high-tech acoustical canopy. I'll bet the National Symphony Orchestra, which calls this place home, must sound fantastic under that canopy.

Another high point was getting to meet Miss Jean

Kennedy Smith at a reception after my performance. Dad told me later that meeting someone from the Kennedy family was like meeting royalty.

People who know me always want to know if I asked her for a kiss. I was wearing a tuxedo, and Mom reminded me several times that this was a formal occasion, so as I thought about it, I thought maybe I'd better not. But in looking back on how warm and welcoming she was, I think it would have been okay. And if I had, I could point to the spot on my cheek and say, "Miss Jean Kennedy Smith," then point to another spot and say, "Oprah," where two of America's royalty had given me a kiss.

DAD

Throughout our lives, there have been numerous times when God's hand reached down at just the right moment. More often than not, we didn't know it was the right moment until we saw it in the rearview mirror. Our experience with the *Extreme Makeover: Home Edition* program is a wonderful example of God's benevolence, his working behind the scenes to make our lives better. Not only that, but this TV program has enabled Patrick Henry to convey his message of love, compassion, and acceptance to millions.

Here's how it all started, and how we ended up with a gorgeous, brand new home.

Patrick Henry and I were in Chicago attending a fund-raiser sponsored by Keshet, an organization that provides educational, recreational, and vocational programs for children and young adults with special needs. Patrick Henry was invited to perform as part of the entertainment after dinner. When he finished, we met a very wealthy man who was quite taken with my son and wanted to help. The gentleman assumed we had some sort of foundation set up, and he wanted to make a generous contribution. But Patrick Henry had no such foundation, so we thanked him very much for his kind gesture. This led to a more serious conversation in which he strongly urged me to set something up for my son. If not a foundation, he thought, we should have a mechanism in place to encourage donations.

I'm always interested in doing things that will benefit my sons, so I investigated. I was told by experts that unless we were going to be dealing with huge sums of money, it probably wouldn't be worthwhile, as it would probably be more of a hassle. Okay, no foundation, but I decided to follow the lead of the man from Chicago and ask for donations on our Web site. I wasn't comfortable asking for a handout, so I tried to word the plea as blandly as possible. At the end, as more or less a joke, I added, "If you are Ty Pennington, or know Ty Pennington, and have discovered our Web site, we could use a home makeover to make our house more accessible for Patrick Henry."

Surprisingly, we received a hefty response from folks who were trying to be helpful. They told us how to apply to *Extreme Makeover: Home Edition* (Ty Pennington is the host) and how to let the show know who we were and why we would be good candidates. (Later, I learned the show had received hundreds of e-mails from strangers telling them about us. I was in utter disbelief. Was that all due to just my Web site posting?) We loved the show and were faithful followers. The idea turned over in my mind whenever I saw Patrick Henry struggling to get around a house that opposed his every action or whenever it happened to be raining and our basement flooded. It seemed wonderful, but it also seemed too good to be true.

Our house had two bedrooms, and when the boys were young, all three shared one room. Then, when Cameron got to the point where he needed to move from the crib to a bed, there wasn't room for it. So, Patricia and I moved into the living room, and we moved Jesse and Cameron into our bedroom. There was only one bathroom, which made things really hectic when we all were trying to get ready to go somewhere. We desperately needed another bedroom and bathroom, and more closet space.

As things progressed we shot a video filming Patrick Henry's difficult journey from the family room back to his bedroom. It was something we were used to seeing him do, but this time it took on a whole new meaning. I felt as though I were watching him go through this for the first time.

When he got to the ramp that leads up to the kitchen, he slid off his wheelchair and started scooting up on his belly, inch by inch, towing the chair behind him. Once he cleared the ramp, he struggled to get back in his chair, then began the arduous task of working his way through the twists and turns of the kitchen and dining room and narrow, slanted hallway. He bounced from one wall to the other, banged into furniture, worked hard to make his way over thick carpet, and finally arrived at his destination. This was tough to watch; I was filled with guilt. I was the world's worst parent. How could I be so callous for allowing my son to go through that every day? Until that moment, I had thought of it as good exercise for Patrick Henry, because otherwise, he gets very little. Maybe it was good exercise, but the process was clearly punishing. From that point on, I no longer slept as long as I could in the mornings or left him out in the family room on his own. I started getting up even earlier, glad to sacrifice more sleep to help make my son's life a little easier.

We prayed we'd be chosen. All along, I had visions of the morning when Ty Pennington might yell through his bullhorn, "Good morning, Hughes family," and change our lives forever. Meanwhile, we would have to wait to find out if we were the lucky family.

I felt like a small child again. Christmas was coming, and Santa might be bringing me the one thing I wanted the most in the whole world. Or, he might not. One minute, I would talk myself into believing we had a good shot at it, and how wonderful it would be. Then the next minute, I'd convince myself it was all just a pipe dream.

We were up and down, up and down, until Patricia came up with a solution to help keep us on an even keel. First, we wouldn't discuss anything with the boys. They knew what was going on, of course, but we did our best to focus on our daily life. And second, we made a pact that the moment one of us started down the path of either extreme optimism or pessimism, the other was to slam on the brakes. Usually, it was me who needed the brakes.

Each day, I mentally marked an X on the calendar. I decided that no matter what, I had a new appreciation for my family.

Yet, I began to feel something deep inside telling me that a blessing was coming. I tried to cancel the thought, but it kept getting stronger. I knew I'd better keep this to myself. I was sure Patricia and the boys were experiencing the same emotional roller coaster.

One morning, Patrick Henry and I were in the middle of singing a James Taylor song, "Sweet Baby James," when we thought we heard something. Our wishful imagination? Jesse and Cameron said no; they thought they heard it, too. We stopped singing and strained to listen.

Sure enough, it was Ty on the bullhorn.

"Good morning, Hughes family!"

Jesse, typically the least emotional one of the family, rushed out the door first and leaped into hugs and high-fives. Cameron was right on his heels. Patricia was next, and Patrick Henry and I brought up the rear. My head was spinning: all these stars standing here in our driveway. I looked around and saw all our family members and friends who had come early to watch, just in case. The news media had been tipped off just as Ty was on his way, which gave them time to get here. It was one big, fat, wonderful circus!

Patrick Henry

I could feel the vibes from Mom and Dad and my brothers. Those vibes were so powerful they about knocked me out of my chair! I've never felt anything like it. Jesse kept saying, "I'm going to get my own room, I'm going to get my own room." All I could think was, *This is really happening to us. I'm going to have a new place to live. I'm going to be able to get around more easily. I'm going to be independent.* I was shaking all over, doing my "happy dance," but everyone else was so beside themselves I doubt they noticed.

Ty Pennington came into the house and interviewed me and Dad. He was so wonderful and thoughtful. He wanted to know all about us, but he was careful not to give us much information in return about what was in store. Each step along the way was meant to be a surprise. Then, he interviewed me separately and asked me how I was feeling and if there was anything he could do for me. My mouth was so dry from the excitement I could barely answer.

We had to be all packed and ready that morning to leave town on vacation. They were sending us away while they rebuilt our home from scratch! Mysteriously, we were told to pack swim trunks and sweaters. We couldn't wait to learn where we'd be going. But before we could find out, Dad, Ty, and I climbed into Dad's van and headed for the University of Louisville.

As part of the home makeover process, we had been asked earlier if there is anything the crew could do for someone else important to us, like an organization that serves others.

So many wonderful organizations came to mind, it was hard to pick just one. But Dad and I decided that Dr. Byrne and the U of L marching band had been so good to us, that if we were selected, we'd want to do something nice for them. I thought about that horrible, mosquito-infested swamp we practiced on. "We should ask for a new field," I told Dad. He thought it was a great idea.

We drove down to U of L and found the whole band there. They had no idea why they'd been gathered, and later, I learned the band members were miffed, thinking that another practice session had been heaped upon them. Instead, it was Ty Pennington—making an announcement that we'd be getting a new field as part of the *Extreme Makeover* program! That sure made everybody happy.

We joined up with Mom, Jesse, and Cameron, and our whole family left for the airport and our flight—to London! I had always wanted to go to England. I couldn't wait to hear Big Ben up close.

It was the last time we would ever see our old home, which I'd lived in ever since I was born. I'm sure Dad said, "Thank goodness, and good riddance." Before our trip, the makeover team had asked us if there were any things we were sure we didn't want in our new home, or wanted to save. I couldn't think of anything in particular. At first, Mom and Dad had a list of things they wanted to keep. These items would need to be stored until our new house was ready. But as my parents thought about it, they decided just to start all over again. They figured that it would be best if everything was new.

Our old house was prone to frequent flooding. Every time we had a heavy rain, poor Dad was constantly down in the basement cleaning up water. For that reason alone, the new home was more of a blessing than we knew at the time. By March, just a few months after we moved in, we had already gotten a full year's worth of rain. It was one of the wettest winters on record. That much rainwater in our old basement would have been waist deep and ruined everything down there. We probably would have had to move our hot-water heater, washer, and dryer upstairs, taking much of that space away.

We arrived in London the next morning, again to camera crews and microphones everywhere. Since everything we did was on film, my brothers and I felt like movie stars. While in London, we received a video from Ty of our house being demo'd. As we sat by the river Thames, using a laptop computer, we watched our house being torn down back in Louisville. I could hear the booming as Dad described the destruction to me: sledgehammers smashing the toilets, sinks, and windows . . . a bulldozer making quick work of the walls . . . the roof spectacularly crashing down and caving in. Pretty awesome how fast everything went.

After our old house was razed, the new home would be built and decorated on the same site, start to finish, in just one week by local contractors and volunteers. All this would occur while we were in London.

Ed, one of the show's designers, happens to be from London and was our tour guide, along with a few other hometown guides who helped out. We visited all the sites: London Bridge, Tower Bridge, the crown jewels, Buckingham Palace, and many others, but for me, the highlight on the tour was the Lyceum Theater. Ed told us about the theater's up-and-down history—destroyed by fire, rebuilt, abandoned, then refurbished in 1994. But the best part was meeting the cast of *The Lion King* backstage. It was one of my favorite movies when I was a kid, and I knew all the characters and their lines by heart. The cast was getting ready to warm up for that evening's performance, and the director asked me if I'd like to help. Sure I would, but I wasn't sure exactly what to do. So, I decided to use the warm-up exercises we performed when I was in the high school chorus. We worked up the scale in half steps to the point where I thought we were getting a little too high, then we came back down. The cast loved it.

Then I asked if I could feel some of the characters in costume and some of the stage props so that I'd have a better idea what was happening during the show. I loved the dress that Nala, the lioness, wore in the show. It was loaded with all different kinds of beads and I loved the feel, but it also had a distinct sound each time she moved. I also felt Zazu, the bird, a red-billed hornbill. He was like a big puppet on poles, and he would fly around when the poles were moved. I wanted to feel some of the faces, but someone explained that I'd probably smudge the makeup, which took a long time to put on and get right.

The next day, we were out again and I finally got to hear Big Ben chime up close and at noon. It wasn't a big deal to anyone else, but to me, it was incredible. At home, I have CDs that are all sound effects, and one of my favorites is "Big Ben Strikes Twelve," recorded from London Tower. It goes for one minute, seventeen seconds, and I've listened to it hundreds of times. Now, actually being here right below it, hearing it and experiencing it, was indescribable. It's like when you idolize a performer and then you finally get to see the person, not only live, but close enough to touch.

When you go on vacation, it usually feels as if the time flies by and it's over too fast. This time, we loved London, but our hearts were in Louisville, anxiously wondering what was happening. Later on, once we were home, family and friends brought us all the newspapers and videotapes of what happened the week we were gone. Our story was on the local TV news every night and on the front page of our newspaper every morning. The stories showed the amazing progress on our new home day by day. Thousands of volunteers working round the clock can do wonders. I still laugh that we missed it all—it's as if we threw the biggest party ever, invited thousands, and then didn't even show up.

It was time to leave, so we flew back to America. Although we were back in the States, we still didn't have a clue what our home might be like. The show had asked us about changes we'd like in our new home, and I had a lot of ideas.

First, I wanted a big garage for the van. In bad weather, I'd have to wait just inside the door of the family room for my wheelchair wheels to dry before going through the house; otherwise, I'd leave wet tracks everywhere. While I waited,

I'd be thinking about all the things I could be doing besides just sitting there. Second on my list was a swimming pool at just the right depth—water up to my chest—which would support me so that I could stand up and walk on the bottom, and a deeper end for jumping in and horsing around. I also wanted a ladder and a chair lift so that I could easily get into and out of the water.

I was anxious to have my own space and have it be accessible to me: a kitchen where I could learn to cook, a bathroom with a shower I could roll into in my wheelchair without assistance, and a walk-in (or in my case, a roll-in) closet. Some new closets have these special clothes racks where all you have to do is pull on a lever and it brings your clothes down to you. Then, when you push the lever back up a little bit, it retracts. That would be great, because I'd be able to get my own clothes without needing help from anyone.

While I was at it, I figured I might as well dream big. So I told them I'd like to have a new piano, my own recording studio, a keyboard with all kinds of special musical effects on it, and a power-driven chair, one where each wheel has a sensor that beeps to warn you if you're going to hit something. But no matter what happened, I was just hoping to be a step closer to being able to live on my own.

Once we got back to Louisville, we began to realize how much coverage there was the week we were gone. Strangers came up to us and wanted to meet us. Dad had to tell them really fast not to tell us any details about the house. So, everyone was great about that. All I heard was, "You'll love it; it's beautiful," and "It'll knock your socks off."

It was so exciting to be back in our hometown. Right away, we took a trip in a limo to an unknown destination. As we got close, we could hear the crowd, and it kept getting louder. I got an inkling of where we were and what was about to happen, and I started to shake. Dad was really excited, too. When we exited the limo, the crowd went crazy. I could hear the whole marching band start playing the Cardinal Fight Song. Dad leaned over to me and told me about all our friends and relatives in the crowd, and he described where we stood—the brand new marching band practice field. "This is all for you," he said.

For the first time in my life, I think, I was speechless. Not only was I so thrilled to be part of this, but I was also so happy for Dr. Byrne and all my friends in the band. Dad wheeled me across the field. It felt amazing—no wobbling, no sinking, and Dad didn't have to pull me back and do a wheelie. The ride was smooth and easy, even though we didn't have the special wheels on the chair.

In the eleven years that Dr. Byrne had been band director at U of L, he and the band had been relocated five times. Five fields, each progressively worse than the previous one. He'd get a field, and then someone higher on the pecking order, a sports team or intramurals, would want it and it would be taken away. But he persevered and always made the marching band members feel that what they were doing was important nonetheless; the quality of the field didn't matter. That's true leadership.

I learned that the new field was level, had beautiful grass, and a ridgeline in the middle for proper drainage. *Hasta la vista,* mud and mosquitoes. The field was painted like a real football field, with accurate markings to give the marchers reference points when going through maneuvers. There was a huge storage building, something we desperately needed, a shelter to allow us to duck in the shade or out of the rain, a nice fence around the whole field, and beautiful landscaping. A big arch covered the entrance, and there was a plaque. They told me to read the plaque; it was in Braille as well as regular print. It proclaimed the "University of Louisville Marching Band Field, inspired by Patrick Henry Hughes." I was giddy at this point, overwhelmed by the many blessings coming our way all at once.

This all had been so tremendous, and we hadn't even seen our new house yet. We were exhausted and elated at the same time.

Thousands of interested people were waiting for us to come home, even arriving many hours early just to reserve a place to stand and see clearly, and despite the pouring rain, the crowd kept growing.

Finally, just when we couldn't stand the excitement any longer, we were headed for our new home. When I felt the car turn, I knew we were coming up our long driveway. The closer we got, the louder the noise rang in our ears. I thought the crowd at the marching band practice field was loud, but that was nothing compared to this. It was deafening. I felt the blood rush to my head.

The limo pulled up. All my family could see was the side of a bus, which blocked the view of our new home.

Then the crowd started chanting the famous phrase, "Move that bus! Move that bus!" Thousands of folks in unison. We got out of the limo and waved to the crowd, which screamed even louder. Now it was time for the big countdown. Time to move that bus!

When they did, Mom and Dad were speechless. Since I couldn't see the reveal, they had me feel it. The crew from Elite Homes of Louisville, along with help from the School of Engineering at U of L, had prepared a plastic model—an exact, to-scale replica of the new house—and placed it in my lap for me to touch. I moved my hands over the model as Dad described what stood in front of him. Our new home style was called the Jamestown, and it was like an English country cottage, all on one floor. Sounds funny, I know, but I actually felt as if I was "seeing" our new home right there with him.

The outside was beautiful, but when we went inside, Mom was beside herself at how it was furnished and decorated. She said it was as if she'd chosen every single detail, it was that perfect. I just couldn't wait to get to my room.

"Room" turned out to be an understatement. I should say my apartment. It had a private entrance and was huge, several rooms together in a single space without walls. I could zoom around in my wheelchair and not hit a thing! That day,

November 7, was my independence day. The doors and appliances are voice activated, so that I can open a door or tell the TV to drop from the ceiling, what channel I want and how loud, by just saying so. Amazing!

We went through my new kingdom step by step. First, I had my own incredible kitchen, where everything is accessible. I can roll right up to the counter, get my knees under it, and reach for whatever I need on the lower-than-usual countertops. In our old kitchen, the footrests of my chair would bang into the cabinets, the stove, or the sink, and I was never able to get close enough to do anything. And even if I could get closer, everything was too high for me to reach. What's more, the old kitchen was set up like a galley, so narrow that only two people at a time could be in there and both had to be standing. It was much too restrictive for me to move around in my wheelchair.

Next was the giant bathroom, with a big shower positioned so I can roll my chair straight into it—Mom and Dad don't have to struggle to lift me into a tub anymore. Off the bathroom was a walk-in closet with fancy, pull-down clothes racks, which alone was bigger than my bedroom in the old house. I had my own TV lounge area with sofa and chairs, and next to it was a top-of-the-line piano, a baby grand. As if that wasn't enough—I couldn't believe it—but in the corner was an actual recording studio with state-of-the-art sound-mixing equipment I was anxious to learn how to use. There was a new computer, scanner, and all sorts of other audio equipment designed to help me study. My bedroom area had a huge bed, with built-in big pocket shelves for all my CDs, videos, and such.

And finally, there was that magical power wheelchair that would sound if an obstacle was in my way—not that I had to worry about that very much in this new, vastly open space.

My room was paradise, and I wanted to stay there and enjoy. But there'd be time for that later. We were off to Jesse's room. He might have been the most excited of all of us; having his own room for the first time was so big for him. Jesse is into photography, and that was the theme of his room—right down to a real photo booth, the kind amusement parks have that take a strip of four photos while you stick your tongue out and act goofy. Meanwhile, the theme of Cameron's room was rock music, with guitars all over the place—on the walls, in stands, and even in the floor with Plexiglas on top.

And, of course, I can't forget to mention the garage, big enough for at least two vans. My waiting for my wheels to dry was a thing of the past.

As all of it soaked in, I said a little prayer, thanking God for this generosity that was way beyond anything I could have dreamed of.

But there was one more surprise to come. In our backyard was a beautiful swimming pool. It was too cold to swim, but I just wanted to jump right in. When summer came, I knew I'd be in there every day, especially those sweltering nights after preseason band camp, playing rounds of Marco Polo with my brothers and practicing my walk.

DAD

As I think about these incredible gifts we have received from the angels at *Extreme Makeover: Home Edition,* I realize how impotent my words are to describe our gratitude or the magnitude of the experience. The crew from the show get very personally involved with various projects in the new home, whether it be conjuring up the theme for each bedroom, or how to decorate the family room to reflect our spirit. We got to know each member of the crew as a friend and hated to see them go. A few months later, when we visited Los Angeles, they had a big surprise for us. Several crew members stopped by or called us, and we relived the excitement of all these wonderful blessings with them. As for our family, we relive that joy in our home every single day.

Love, Given Freely, Multiplies and Returns

PATRICK HENRY

Love is the most powerful energy in the world, so powerful it cannot be governed by scientific laws. When I think about all the love that has been poured on us in Nashville, at Fan Fair and the Grand Ole Opry; the love from all my teachers and Miss Hinda, especially; from Dr. Byrne and my marching band friends; and the ultimate, our experience with the crew from *Extreme Makeover: Home Edition,* I believe we have received so much more love than we have ever given out.

My music is a gift I can share. It's so much a part of me, when I play I feel like I'm sharing myself with whoever is there listening. I hope the audience can feel the love I'm sending. It comes back to me and accumulates into an irresistible force; I feel like I can accomplish anything.

Thousands of volunteers banded together to bring about our new home, donating their time, energy, and resources to create something they knew would make an incredible difference in my life. I have always dreamed of being more independent and less of a burden on others, but I didn't see how this would be possible, given my family's circumstances. But love found a way, connecting with the *Extreme Makeover* folks, setting into motion an act of generosity so big, it has made my dreams come true.

So, please, invest your love in others, knowing it pays compound interest that will reward you, the giver, many times over and in more ways than you can imagine.

Chapter 8

Live Each Day
Like the Last Day of
Summer Vacation

*Who of you by worrying
can add a single hour to his life?*
—MATTHEW 6:27

PATRICK HENRY

You know when you were a kid and you had all summer to fool around, then suddenly you realized it had slipped away? It was your last day of freedom before school started again. You'd think about all the things you wish you had done, and you'd try to cram in as many as you could. You'd try to savor every minute. That's how we should always live. When you don't pay attention, today becomes yesterday before you're ready.

I don't like to spend too much time sleeping. I'm afraid I might miss something. Often, when Dad and I are invited to speak and perform somewhere, we might be told that just

199

prior to our appearance at the main event, we also have the opportunity to meet with a smaller group at a location just down the road. Dad wants to say no, because we'll be tired from traveling and he thinks we should take a nap. I always want to go to both places so that I can meet as many people as possible. I'll sing him the country song, "Like I said, like I said, I can sleep when I'm dead." He'll groan, but he usually takes me.

I believe in living for the present—focusing my mind on what's happening at this exact moment. When you do, you can enjoy life more fully, because your mind is free from the relentless burdens of worry and fear. Zen practitioners call this problem a "monkey mind," when you subconsciously keep jumping from one thought to the next and get yourself wound up. Mindfulness is all about right now.

Many people have asked me how I adopted this philosophy. It probably comes from a couple places. Like everyone else, I have responsibilities like school, studying, practice. But it also takes me longer to complete just about every task in daily life. If there's something I can't do for myself, I have to be patient and wait for someone to help me. When you add it all up, I don't have much free time to do what I love, and I sure don't want to waste any of it worrying about what might—or might not—happen next.

The other thing that fosters mindfulness is being blind.

When you're blind, the here and now becomes not only more obvious but also more important. You have to focus completely on each action, no matter how small, to get anything done. Imagine something as simple as picking up a spoon. Most people can think, *I need a spoon,* and grab it from the table in a second. I have to concentrate, recall, and process a lot of information to find the spoon quickly without having to grope all over the place. Like, did I hear Mom set it down on my right or my left? Or did she put a bunch of spoons in the middle of the table? Then, when I locate it, I have to feel it and determine which end is the handle. And, since my hands don't work quite the way they're supposed to, it takes time to position the spoon just right in my hand so that I can eat with it. With sight, you'd automatically grab the spoon and eat. You would locate it mindlessly—which frees your mind to constantly be ruminating about other things.

We all have dues of one sort or another to pay, and they're different from one person to the next—even among folks who seem to be similar, like blind people. People who are visually impaired but who could once see have memories of what things look like. When someone says, "There goes a big black dog, or a red fire truck," they can imagine it. I can't do that. On the other hand, folks whose eyesight has degenerated have lost something precious to them. I haven't lost anything. It's hard to say, but I don't think it's a matter of which is worse. I prefer to think about the ways each are best.

You can always think of your circumstances as good or bad. I choose to see my blindness not as a disability, but as an ability.

Here's one way: I can't form opinions based on looks. When you study history, it seems that a lot of problems are caused by snap judgments made about people just on appearance. Maybe their skin is black, brown, yellow, or white. Maybe their clothes are torn or they wear Armani suits. They're overweight or too short, or they have a big nose or bad teeth. Because I can't observe any of these things, to me everyone I meet is perfectly human, the way God created us. And since I'm not influenced by what I can't see, it allows me to tune in to other more important things, like the good that lives inside everyone. I believe everyone is capable of loving and being loved.

My parents warned me that some people I meet may make assumptions about me because I'm in a wheelchair—like that I'm helpless or unintelligent—in a way they wouldn't if we were just talking on the phone for the first time. But it's easy to judge based on an impression, not on what we know to be true. Mom says she does this, too, without realizing it.

Once, Mom and a colleague were in Boston for a convention and were having coffee in the coffee shop of the hotel. Sitting close by was a guy with a spiked Mohawk, lots of facial piercings, and tattoos everywhere. Her colleague saw him and scoffed. Mom gave him a look, too, and admits her first thought was, "Yuk!" But then she suddenly thought to herself, what if Patrick Henry were here and heard us talking about him? He'd probably want to go over immediately and say, "Hello, my name's Patrick Henry Hughes. What's yours?" (I have a habit of introducing myself to strangers wherever we go.) She decided to do something she normally wouldn't do. When she caught his eye, she asked if he was with the convention. He wasn't, but it turned out he was quite a talker and they all ended up having a conversation. She left there that day thinking he was one of the nicest, most gentle men she had ever met.

I think I have an advantage when it comes to communicating, too. Take something as simple as a conversation. The average person has to deal with how the other person looks and is dressed, the body language and facial expressions—all coming at you the same time as the words. That's a lot of information to interpret, and I'll bet it's easy to be distracted or misunderstood. I only have the words and tone of voice to go on, which makes conversations more direct for me.

Okay, I know what you must be thinking. I'm putting a positive spin on my blindness. You probably think that someone like me would desire eyesight more than anything. I'm definitely curious, but I'm not sure I'd trade. What would I do if a surgeon said, "Patrick Henry, I could perform an operation on you for free, and it's guaranteed to be safe and to give you sight, but you have to decide if you want it today"? (Of course, no such transplant surgery for my condition yet exists.) Dad would strongly encourage me to have it. But honestly, I'd need more time to think about it.

On our trips, Dad and I have talked about this quite a lot. When I consider the pros of it, the ability to see would certainly help me live more independently, and that's really important to me. But, on the other side, since I don't really know what it means to see, if I suddenly had this ability, I'd probably be shocked. I don't have images of what anything looks like, but I carry around a "brain idea" about things and this helps me interpret the world. If I could suddenly see, everything I think I know and have learned over the last twenty years would be turned upside down.

I have to admit, I've often wondered what vision might be like, or at least what it would be like to have some visual memories. Anyone would be curious, I'm sure, about things they are aware of but have never experienced. That's why people take trips to Egypt to see the great Pyramids, or to London to see Big Ben. The difference for me is I have missed seeing infinitely more things than the average sighted person has. What does a lunar eclipse look like, a field of tulips blooming, the Grand Canyon? What about man-made structures like a skyscraper, the Statue of Liberty, or Papa John's Cardinal football stadium, where we march at halftime? I have no idea. But I don't dwell on it. As Mom would say when I was young, "That's the 'poor-me way,' and we don't think like that around here." I'm lucky Mom helped me shape my attitude about life right from the start. Why fret that I don't know what things look like? Why not turn it around and say, few people on the planet have ever known what I perceive every day in my mind's eye? It's unique and perfect, and I wish I could share it with you, just like you might want to share the sighted world with me.

We all can discover beauty in our own ways.

I try to squeeze every bit of life I can into every day, and that includes long phone conversations with Ashley, my girlfriend. We shared a close relationship through high school and saw each other every day. Now that we live about a forty-five-minute drive apart, meeting up on the phone is about the best we can do most of the time. Ashley has had vision problems from birth and can see only dim shadows, nothing that really helps her see what's going on in the world, so we have a lot in common in that regard.

We had met years before at summer camp, but hadn't really talked until one day over lunch in the Atherton High School cafeteria. She said she was impressed by my piano skills; I liked the way she sang. She told me she was going to be in the school choir and her goal was to someday be a choir director. She also told me she thought I had a great singing voice. From that point on, I knew we'd be close friends.

As our relationship grew, I realized how great it was having someone to talk to about things I couldn't discuss in the same way, as a blind person, with anyone else. She had a different vision coach than I did, and we'd compare notes on what our coaches did to help us learn—my coach was taking me places, exposing me to things I could really experience by smelling, touching, and hearing. Ashley and I would talk about everything that was going on at school, and she'd always know immediately what I was feeling, because she was thinking the same things.

We also happen to have many of the same interests. Ashley not only loves country music, but loves classical music, too. When she listens to classical music at home, she cranks up the volume the way other people listen to heavy metal—so loud it loosens your teeth. Ashley's dream was to appear on *American Idol;* I told her to go for it.

In high school, we always had a good time together, whether we were going to birthday parties, church outings, or just visiting each other's house, where we'd sit around and talk, or I'd play music for her. I remember when she asked me what I thought she looked like. Dad says to be careful when a girl asks you something like that, because it can get you into trouble. But I didn't have to worry. "You're very pretty," I said, and I meant it.

One night, we were at a Christmas party and we started talking. I was telling her that I had heard a little about a new hip surgery. I didn't know if I was even a candidate for it, but what if one day in the future I might be able to walk? Or even stand? When she asked me if I'd like to be able to, I said, "Sure!" Then she got quiet, and I thought I had said something wrong. Finally, she said: "Patrick Henry, I like you in your wheelchair." I loved that she liked me just the way I am.

We had the best time at our Junior Prom. I don't know who was more excited, Ashley or her older sister, who fixed Ashley's hair and got her all dolled up for the night. I do have to admit that at such times, I'd like to have a glimpse of her, something to hold on to in my mind, because everyone was making such a fuss over her. But I thought instead about how much fun we were going to have.

My tuxedo was a challenge to fit—there was a lot of measuring going on, and it took a while to do all the alterations. But when I was dressed, Dad said I looked pretty good. It was the first time I ever wore a vest. It was velvet and smooth to the touch.

At the prom, we danced quite a bit. Ashley loves to dance. Like most guys, I can take it or leave it, but I wanted to make her happy. She wheeled me onto the dance floor, and I held her hand. Thankfully, she did all the work—all I had to do was move my shoulders around and shimmy a little bit. But it was fun and I loved to hear her laugh while we danced.

The next year, we went to the prom as seniors, which was really cool. We found a piano, and Ashley wanted me to serenade her. I pretended I didn't want to, but I really couldn't wait, so I gave in pretty fast. We had a blast playing all sorts of songs, singing and just acting silly. That was a great night.

I'm often asked about my future, particularly with Ashley. She's a very special person to me. What do I think will happen? Maybe we'll get married and live happily ever after. The reality of this, of course, is way in the future. Both of us have a lot to accomplish to reach our goals and realize our dreams in the years ahead.

In elementary school, I went to a Spanish immersion school, meaning that the language is sprinkled throughout the entire curriculum. We'd learn our colors or numbers in English, then we'd learn them in Spanish. When we first started, I didn't think much one way or the other about learning Spanish, until I heard my new teacher speak in her Chilean accent. I was only in kindergarten at the time, but I was hooked. It gave me goose bumps, and I decided right then I wanted to be able to speak Spanish fluently.

In the beginning, language classes can be a struggle—it takes a lot of effort to put together a sentence that makes sense. But the classes do help you live mindfully. When you start learning Spanish, you can't yet think in Spanish, so you have to concentrate on every individual word and what it means. You can't allow your mind to wander ahead as you do in your native language, thinking about how you'll finish a sentence, or what you expect the other person might say. Learning another language forces you to be in the moment.

I worked hard on my lessons, always making them my priority, and soon I felt comfortable having a conversation, although I did have some trouble with rolling my Rs off my tongue. Throughout school, I concentrated my efforts on Spanish classes whenever I could, went on to take advanced Spanish in high school, and then tested out of two years of Spanish at the University of Louisville.

We have a lot of Spanish-speaking people in this country today, and knowing Spanish allows me to meet new friends who I'd miss otherwise. In 2001, we took a vacation trip to Washington, D.C., and I tried to talk Dad into taking me to the Mexican embassy to practice my Spanish. He thought it was crazy to interrupt those people's workday just so I could speak Spanish with them, but Mom intervened. What could it hurt? And besides, we were on vacation. Dad finally gave in, but he made it clear I wasn't to hang out for too long and make a nuisance of myself.

Mom wheeled me into the embassy and up to the receptionist. "Have at it," she said.

"*Perdoname,*" I said. (Excuse me.)

"*¿Si?*" the receptionist replied. (Yes?)

"*¿Cómo se llama?*" (What's your name?) It's always the first thing I ask anyone.

"Rosaura," she said in the prettiest voice, which sounded like a melody.

"*Me llamo Patricio, mucho gusto.*" (My name is Patrick, nice to meet you.)

Then I asked, "*¿Por cuánto tiempo ha estado en los Estados Unidos?*" (How long have you been in the United States?)

We were off and running, *hablando el Español,* talking in Spanish about Mexico and her experiences growing up there as a little girl. I kept asking her questions, and she'd respond in great detail, the words fluttering. After a while, Mom whispered to me that we'd better go and quit bothering her. But she said, "No bother, *Señora,* my pleasure." So I kept chatting as long as I could.

I have traveled to two Spanish-speaking countries, Ecuador and Spain. My first big trip was to Ecuador, with my high school choir when I was a sophomore, and I was so excited and anxious to talk to anyone who would talk to me. Fortunately, we stayed with a host family in Quito, which gave me a lot of conversation practice. Our choir performed at great cathedrals all over the country, and because I could speak the language, I'd introduce the songs we were going to sing and give some background. When the Ecuadorians saw that I could speak their language, they mobbed me.

I love to travel, which may seem strange since I can't sight-see and because traveling usually is a big hassle, especially by air. The seats don't fit me right, and a long flight is really uncomfortable and fatiguing. Getting there might not be much fun, but being there sure is, and it more than makes up for any problems en route.

Even though I can't see anything, I feel the ambiance of a place. I particularly listen for the sounds: conversations, horns, sirens, shoes clopping along on cobblestones, shouts from vendors, church bells, local music. Everything I hear gives me a unique sense of each town or city. I like to record all these sounds and play them back when I get home so I can relive the moments in the same way sighted folks take lots of pictures.

DAD

Patrick Henry has always been very disciplined in his approach to everything he does—from the time he was a baby. When he would play with his toys, he'd do it the same way every time, as if following a script. He'd place the basket beside him, take out one toy, feel it, do whatever it took to create the noise it made by squeezing, pulling, or chewing it, enjoy the sound it made until he had had enough, then gently set it aside and moved on to the next toy. I never saw him dump his toys out or grab several at a time; that would be against his established procedure.

Today, he brings that same careful discipline to his music

and schoolwork. He always has a clock to time his afternoon practice sessions, usually for one hour on weekdays and two on weekends and during the summer months. If we didn't time him, he'd never quit and get other things done. One afternoon, I left to pick up some doughnuts and realized I hadn't left a clock for him. When I came back, I was teasing when I asked him, "How long have you been playing?" because I knew he didn't have a way to time himself. He paused for just a moment, then said, "Twenty-eight minutes." He was exactly right. He had been playing Bach and some other classical pieces, but I couldn't imagine how he knew the precise time. "I had the metronome set for one hundred counts per minute," he said, "and all I had to do was keep track of the count—two thousand eight hundred." If this was anyone else, I'd be looking for the hidden clock.

Patrick Henry is on the five-year plan at the University of Louisville, because he can manage only twelve credits per term rather than the sixteen it takes to graduate in four years. This is due to his extensive travel schedule, public appearances around his hometown, and the extra time involved in participating with the marching band. He's majoring in Spanish and plans to use his language skills professionally, perhaps in the State Department, working in the ambassador core in some way in a Spanish-speaking country.

Over the years, I've come to appreciate the value of focus and living in the moment. I've also become aware of how much more of that I do naturally because of my son. When we are at the airport and we have to get from the van to the ticket desk, I have to push Patrick Henry while I tug a suitcase behind and manage a carry-on bag. This juggling act takes every ounce of concentration I can muster. My son always volunteers to push the suitcase in front, but since he can't see or anticipate problems, like a one-inch rise in the concrete, he can't avoid jackknifing. On the football field at halftime, I have to be completely immersed in what I'm doing, as the slightest miscue could lead to a disaster of major proportions.

Having applied this type of single-mindedness to most of my dealings nowadays, I find that it really helps reduce the stress. Stay with just one thing, and see it through to the end or at least as far as possible, before moving on to the next. In the old days, I'd always be multitasking like crazy, and it drove me *crazy*. Just setting up everything that needs to be done for one of Patrick Henry's appearances is pretty much a full-time job. Getting the right seat on the airplane so that his discomfort is minimized as much as possible, making sure we can rent a van (because a car can't accommodate my son and his chair), navigating to a hotel in a strange city, and on and on. Going through airport security requires double patience, undoing and then redoing our personal items for both of us. If I didn't break everything up into simple, single steps the way my son does, I'd be a wreck by the time we got anywhere. Taking life one moment at a time really helps.

PATRICK HENRY

When you're young and you think about what your job might be in the future, your parents always like to hear that you are interested in doing something practical, something that will pay the bills. Well, I have my "practical" dreams: working for the State Department, performing music, becoming a motivational speaker. But I also have my secret passion that, in the best of all worlds, would be my vocation for life.

My ultimate goal is to host a TV game show. Not one of the ones currently on the air, but one of my own creation. I've had lots of ideas for how the game might go and what name it might have, though I'm not going to share these ideas just yet. My plan is to live at home in my wonderful, new "in house" apartment. Oprah has shown us that you don't have to relocate to New York or Los Angeles and that you can do things in your own hometown, the way she did. So I hope to duplicate her example and hit it big from Louisville. Once my game show is well established, I have another goal: to be the longest-running TV game show host in history and beat Mr. Bob Barker's record of fifty-one years.

What I'm going to do for the rest of my life is an important decision, but I don't spend a lot of time dealing with it, because I don't want it to take away from what's going on in my life right now. I've just finished my second year of college, and I'm looking forward to three more great years. A big part of that will be spent as a proud member of the University of Louisville marching band.

Game days have become something really special in my life. Growing up, I was never much of a sports fan. But attending home football games as a part of the University of Louisville marching band, being right in the center of everything, has changed that in a big way.

Dad and I have marched in more than a dozen home games, and several have been nationally televised. We also marched in the biggest game in U of L football history, the Orange Bowl. That was really incredible, but nothing can compare with the excitement of that first game. I've relived that day, September 3, 2006, in my mind so many times, it's like a dear old friend.

I don't know what to expect, but I'm already excited. Papa John's Cardinal Stadium is empty. It's 2:30, 4-1/2 hours before the 7:00 P.M. kickoff for the first game of the season, against our bitter in-state rival, the University of Kentucky Wildcats.

For the first time, I'm wearing my black pants—they're like bib overalls—and my red marching-band T-shirt. My band jacket is really hot in warm weather, and because today is so hot, I hope I won't have to put it on until it begins to cool down a little.

The first thing we do is gather into concert arcs in the middle of the field. The first arc has eight band members; the next, twelve; the next, twenty; and so on. We warm up for about thirty minutes, performing scales and exercises.

For the next hour, we do marching drills. Dr. Byrne and the drum major watch us closely and help us be sure to stay in formation and do the right things, like keeping our knees up and positioning our instruments so that the sound carries over the walls and well up into the stands. Dr. Byrne reminds us: "You perform like you practice, so you can't get sloppy."

Dad and I are intently focused on every drill, especially since it's our first real live experience. He's like the quarterback who studies the plays again, the formations we'll employ on the field. He's the one who has to follow the leads and make sure our movements are in sync and perfectly timed, just like throwing to a wide receiver going out on a pass route. I'm in charge of the music and have to be aware of all the cues and stay focused on exactly when I'm supposed to pitch in. Actually, we're getting off easy, because we get to split the duties. The rest of the band members have to do both at the same time.

At four o'clock, it's time to put on our band jackets, our hats with the plumes, and our white gloves. It's hot, but I'm so excited, it doesn't matter. We form rows of four and get ready for our drum-line march around the outside of the stadium. We march by the tailgaters, who cheer us like the crazy fans they are, and we love it. Then we march down to where the football team will be arriving.

Even though it's a home game, all the players come in

together on buses from the athletic dorms. We play the Cardinal Fight Song as they get off the buses in their street clothes. The cheering fans have formed a long corridor leading from the parking lot to the stadium, and as the players make their way through the corridor, we follow along behind them. We're supposed to face straight ahead and not break ranks, but Dad leans over me and says; "Reach out, Son, they want to meet you." I do, and the fans shake my hand and pat me on the back. I wasn't expecting that. Finally, we march off and continue all the way around the stadium, past more tailgaters, and enter the stadium where we left.

We make necessary adjustments, fix broken valves on instruments, adjust chinstraps, replace mouthpieces. Our last duty prior to kickoff is to leave the stadium again and visit the president's tent, where all the dignitaries hang out. We play the Fight Song and other selections for them, and then we return to the stadium to play for the fans as they file into their seats.

At about ten minutes before kickoff, all 220 band members get in line and wait for the word to move out. Dad and I are at the end of the line as we head toward the "crunch zone," the end zone on the south end of the stadium. This is where the loudest and craziest fans sit; Dad had season tickets there for years, along with lots of our friends. We're moving along at a fairly rapid pace, and as we near the goalposts, I hear the crowd up ahead getting louder. Dad puts his hand on my shoulder and says, "Get ready, Son." From the tone of his voice, something big is going on up ahead. We slow to a crawl.

The fans get up from their seats and get as close to the

field as they can, lining up shoulder to shoulder, squeezing in along the rail, all the way around. Many hundreds more pack in behind them, two and three deep. Dad tells me to raise my hand as far as I can. Rabid fans lean over the rails to slap high-fives. "We love you, Patrick!" "Way to go!" "God bless you!" I'm speechless, and all I can do is smile up at them. It's awesome!

As we move along making our way through the crunch zone and toward the visitors' sideline, the din grows louder. It seems as if everyone in the world is there trying to greet us and touch us. I feel like I'm floating right up out of my seat. *This is how a rock star must feel,* I think. Dad and I linger a bit longer, touching every hand we can, as the rest of the band makes its way back to our seats. My arm is tired from holding it up, but I don't want it to end.

With the exception of the Kentucky Derby, the annual football game between the two big state universities— University of Louisville and University of Kentucky—is the biggest event in the state each year. The winner claims bragging rights until the two schools meet on the basketball court months later. The rivalry is even bigger and more spirited in the city of Louisville, because the fan base is split between the two schools. When folks go to work on Monday morning, they will either dish it out to losing fans or be prepared to swallow a lot of teasing. Sometimes, families have split loyalties, husbands against wives, brothers against brothers, like in the Civil War, and Dad tells me it's common to see a husband in Cardinal red and the wife in Wildcat blue. It's pretty intense, especially with tickets so hard to come by.

The tension keeps building as fans pour into the stadium. Dad describes for me how the Cardinal bird mascot is making his way down in a parachute and landing, hopefully at midfield. "We're at three minutes. Two minutes forty-five. Two minutes thirty seconds," Dad narrates for me the big clock in the end zone, counting down the minutes to game time. Finally, the song "Prepare for Battle" begins to rumble, and the big screen in the end zone shows the players coming out of the locker room and down the long hallway, marching two abreast, their game faces on.

The players come through the door and into the stadium and gather behind the goal posts in the north end zone. They wait to dash through a thick machine-made veil of smoke. To heighten anticipation, now Metallica's deep, pounding bass drums reverberate through the stadium. The ominous beat penetrates your heart and makes you want to scream, and I do. Football is like war—everyone psyched up, adrenalin pouring out. I now understand sports mania, how a game is so much more than just an athletic contest to the fans in the stands.

After we play the national anthem, the bands from both schools join on the field to play "My Old Kentucky Home," a song reserved for very special occasions only, like as the horses start moving toward the gate for the Kentucky Derby. The bands intermingle—all the trumpets from both bands gather together, all the drummers, and so on—alternating Cardinal red with Wildcat blue as a sign of unity and friendship. Forty-five thousand fans are on their feet, waiting for us to begin. I'm excited, but I'm nervous, too. Our first game ever, and my mouth is so dry I hope I can play a note. Too late to worry about that now.

All the fans sing along in unison, Louisville and Kentucky fans united one last time before the kickoff. It's a magical song so packed with emotion for native Kentuckians.

Weep no more, my lady,
Oh weep no more today!
We will sing one song for the old Kentucky home,
For the old Kentucky home far away.

When the music ends, the crowd noise moves to a fever pitch. No more unity and goodwill. It's time for war.

The bands split apart, and we return to our seats. The kickoff is moments away, and the crowd is going nuts. For us, we can rest and finally relax a little while until our big moment arrives.

It's halftime. Both Dad and I take a deep breath as he pushes my wheelchair onto the field. Dad whispers in my ear; "It's showtime. This is what it's all about!"

Soon Dr. Byrne will give the signal and we'll be off. In an instant, the music will intensify by a factor of more than two hundred. Dad will zip me along: stopping abruptly, peeling out, stopping, peeling out again, pivoting, reversing course. I'll be playing my heart out.

Throughout my life, I can't say I had cared about being on

a team of any sort. But today, on this football field, I feel like a warrior. I'm bigger than anything I could be alone. As someone who lives in a world that is largely separate from the world of others, it's so meaningful to be an integral part of this world, a true team member who contributes just like all the rest. I'm thankful to Dad for making it happen, for Dr. Byrne, and for my bandmates, who have accepted me as one of their own.

Just a few years ago, none of this seemed possible. Now, I mesh perfectly, part of an intricate formation. I can't help but feel that anything can happen.

Dad taps me on the shoulder, giving me my cue. The butterflies are doing the rumba in my stomach. In this moment, I feel more blessed and more alive than ever.

I raise my trumpet to my lips.

I am potential.

Live Each Day Like the Last Day of Summer Vacation

PATRICK HENRY

How many todays do you have left in your life? If you are like me, twenty years old, and if you aim to reach at least eighty-two, you have 22,645 todays left. That's a big number, but since we don't know God's plan for us, the actual quantity could be far less. What's more, those first twenty years have flashed by—7,305 todays that have vanished into yesterdays. So the challenge is to not let even one day escape without doing something you are proud of.

One waking day is composed of 57,600 seconds. When we pause on just a few of these seconds, we cease to take for granted all the things God does for us constantly. Consider a simple act like breathing. What could be less significant? And yet, if it's taken away, it becomes the most important thing in life. How many miracles of daily life do we overlook because we are multitasking, worrying, caught in trivial arguments?

We weren't intended to live this way. We are meant to have lives that are joyful and fulfilled. I try to focus on the present, even when confronting my daily obligations, like getting ready in the morning, or tackling things I'd rather not, like studying geometry. It's easier being mindful when I have "my time," playing the piano. But what you are doing is less important than *how* you are doing it. Each moment is special in its own way, to be valued and treated with respect.

Today is full of opportunities to do something worthwhile. We all have gifts to share, whether we know it or not. Maybe your abilities are so unique, so different, that you haven't even recognized them. I believe God gave me blindness so that I might see the inner qualities within everyone I meet. I believe He gave me a passion for music to show me what is possible. And He gave me a loving family who helps me in so many ways, so that we might bless each other by giving freely to one another. When you share your unique gifts, you discover the path to your potential—the plan God had for you from the moment you were born.

So, live now, give now, love now, and laugh as much as you can. In the words of one of my heroes, Mother Teresa:

"Yesterday is gone. Tomorrow has not yet come. We have only today. Let us begin."

Resources

Genetic and Rare Diseases (GARD) Information Center
P.O. Box 8126
Gaithersburg, MD 20898-8126
(301) 519-3194
(888) 205-2311 (toll-free)
(240) 632-9164 (fax)
gardinfo@nih.gov
http://www.genome.gov/10000409

Keshet
617 Landwehr Rd.
Northbrook, IL 60062
(847) 205-1234
(847) 480-9120 (fax)
www.keshet.org

MAPS (Microphthalmia Anophthalmia Parent Support)
http://www.maparentsupport.com

National Library Service for the Blind and Physically Handicapped (NLS)
http://www.loc.gov/nls

Kentucky Talking Book Library
P.O. Box 818
Frankfort, KY 40602
(502) 564-8300, ext. 276

(800) 372-2968 (toll-free)
http://www.kdla.ky.gov/libsupport/ktbl.htm

National Organization for Rare Disorders (NORD)
55 Kenosia Avenue
P.O. Box 1968
Danbury, CT 06813-1968
(203) 744-0100
(800) 999-6673 (toll-free/voice mail only)
(203) 798-2291 (fax)
www.rarediseases.org

Recording for the Blind & Dyslexic (RFB&D)
National Headquarters
20 Roszel Road
Princeton, NJ 08540
(866) RFBD-585 (866-732-3585)
(800) 221-4792 (Member Services)
http://www.rfbd.org

Kentucky Unit
240 Haldeman Avenue
Louisville, KY 40206
(502) 895-9068
(502) 897-1145 (fax)
http://www.rfbd.org/Kentucky_Unit.htm

Shriners Hospitals for Children
International Headquarters
2900 Rocky Point Dr.
Tampa, FL 33607
(813) 281-0300

(800) 237-5055 (toll-free)
http://www.shrinershq.org

United Way
http://www.liveunited.org

Metro United Way, Inc.
334 E. Broadway
P.O. Box 4488
Louisville, KY 40204-0488
http://www.metrounitedway.org

**University of Louisville
Marching Band**
Dr. Greg Byrne, Director
University of Louisville
School of Music
Louisville, KY 40292
http://louisville.edu/music/bands/band.html

Visually Impaired Preschool Services
1906 Goldsmith Lane
Louisville, KY 40218
(502) 636-3207
(888) 636-8477 (toll-free)
(502) 636-0024 (fax)
info@vips.org
www.vips.org

VSA arts
818 Connecticut Ave. NW, Suite 600
Washington, DC 20006

(202) 628-2800
(800) 933-8721 (toll-free)
(202) 429-0868 (fax)
info@vsarts.org
http://www.vsarts.org

VSA arts of Kentucky
515 E. 10th
Bowling Green, KY 42101
(270) 781-0872
(877) 417-9594 (toll-free)
(270) 781-8725 (fax)
director@vsartsky.org
http://www.vsartsky.org

WHAS Crusade for Children
P. O. Box 1100
Louisville, KY 40201
(502) 582-7706
(502) 582-7712 (fax)
admin@whascrusade.org
http://www.whascrusade.org

Acknowledgments

First, we thank God and His angels, who repeatedly removed obstacles, always acting at exactly the right moment to bring about exactly the right solution to whatever problems we confronted, transforming seemingly impossible circumstances into profound blessings.

We are thankful to family members who make life worthwhile and help make Patrick Henry's life possible. Patricia, the gentle but powerful force that keeps things moving always in the right direction, the glue that holds it all together. Jesse and Cameron, whose love and support every day is more important to us than they could ever imagine. Granny and Granddaddy, who stepped up and took over at a critical time and kept on giving all they had and loving unconditionally. Mammaw Betty and Granny Flener for their strong work ethic, determination, and loving dedication to family, which provided Patricia the tools to be the kind of mom Patrick Henry needed.

Dr. Greg Byrne, who carried out God's plan for us—a plan that has led to so many unbelievable blessings—and the members of the University of Louisville marching band, who accepted us immediately and unconditionally.

Anita Curpier Stamford, whose vision and insistence that Bryant should write a book about us, was the catalyst that got us all moving. We are indebted to Bryant Stamford, for his intuition, insight, friendship, and tireless efforts in meeting impossible deadlines and keeping a good sense of humor throughout. Amy Hughes, our literary agent, has been an angel to this book and to us personally, making it all happen and staying close by, helping in every way needed, every step of the way. Katie McHugh, our editor, raises editing to an art form, going way beyond the call of duty. Her belief in this book was obvious from day one, and she has spared no effort to make it the best it can be.

Patrick Henry's teachers, administrators, and assistants throughout elementary, middle, and high school were fantastic and contributed to Patrick Henry's growth and quality of life in so many ways. Special thanks to Nettie Wolfe, Kevin Howard, David May, and Viola Garvin for their unending and tireless support on a daily basis.

We would have been helpless and lost without the generous guidance from Visually Impaired Preschool Services, which took us by the hand and led us safely through the gauntlet that was Patrick Henry's earliest years. The Crusade for Children helped us in many ways, too, and served as the launching pad for Patrick Henry's public life. Deana Scoggins paved the way for Patrick Henry's early piano achievements and then graciously passed him along to Hinda Ordman, Patrick Henry's beloved "Little Matzo Ball." Special thanks also to Patrick Henry's trumpet teachers, Arthur Luker (middle school), Sarah McClave (high school), and now Dr. Michael Tunnell, who adds lessons for Patrick Henry to his already full slate of college students.

We thank Byron Crawford for taking an interest in us and writing a wonderful story in his column for the *Louisville Courier-Journal*. Our story then went nationwide in Rick Riley's *Sports Illustrated* column, which led to special features by ESPN, *ABC World News with Charles Gibson,* and, ultimately, to the Disney Wide World of Sports Spirit Award.

We so much appreciate the kindness and attention we have received from so many accomplished performers who are never too busy to take time for us. They include Lane Brody, Richie McDonald of Lone Star, and, of course, Pam Tillis, whose generosity knows no bounds.

It's not possible to express enough thankfulness to the folks associated with ABC's *Extreme Makeover: Home Edition* program. The entire experience was otherworldly, beyond comprehension; it has changed our lives incredibly and for the better. Thanks to Elite Homes (especially owners Joe and Rocky Pusateri), which took on this project, and the multitude of other businesses, civic organizations, and individual volunteers who made it happen. The entire *Extreme Makeover* production team, the stars of the show, and the staff were all wonderful and are amazing for what they do around the country for families like ours.

God bless.

A descendant of the types of Claude Garamond, Sabon was designed by Jan Tschichold in 1964 and jointly released by Stempel, Linotype, and Monotype foundries. The roman design is based on a Garamond specimen printed by Konrad F. Berner, who was married to the widow of another printer, Jacques Sabon. The italic design is based on types by Robert Granjon, a contemporary of Garamond's. This elegant, highly readable typeface is excellent for sophisticated uses ranging from book design to corporate identity.